International Regulation
of Natural Health Products

John Robert Harrison

Universal Publishers
Boca Raton

International Regulation of Natural Health Products

Universal Publishers
Boca Raton, Florida • USA
2008

ISBN-10: 1-58112- 982-3
13-ISBN: 978-1-58112-982-3

Cover design by Shereen Siddiqui

www.universal-publishers.com

This book is dedicated to my wife, Barbara L. Harrison and our sons, William R. L. Harrison and Edward J. Harrison.

The financial assistance of the Natural Health Products Directorate (NHPD), Health Canada is recognized for the support of this research.

TABLE OF CONTENTS

CHAPTER 1

INTRODUCTION TO THE ISSUE

1.1   STATEMENT OF THE ISSUE

The overall objective of this study is to review the natural health product laws and regulations for Canada's primary natural health products (NHP) trading partners, namely, Australia, China, France, Germany, Hong Kong, India, USA, United Kingdom, and the European Union and identify priority areas where policy research should be focussed and then propose strategies to address these selected policy research areas.

The objective of the first phase of this study was to complete a literature and legislative review of the identified NHP regulatory components for countries that comprise Canada's main NHP trading partners. The objective of the second phase of this study was to compare and contrast these regulatory frameworks with that of Canada's NHP Regulations. The second phase reviews the initially collected information and directly compares the findings for other countries with the legislation and regulations covering NHPs in Canada. For this comparison a method was selected in which each identified topic in the Canadian NHP Regulations is compared with those of the other countries. Such an approach facilitates the identification of data gaps, areas of concerns in the legislation of Canada's main trading partners, and of areas requiring further scientific study.

The objective of the third phase of the study consists of a strategy approach which sets out prioritized policy research needs that take into consideration the prior phases of this research.

In preparing this strategy approach, strategic objectives were first developed for the prioritized policy research needs for the Natural Health Products Directorate (NHPD), Health Canada and these objectives were:

- the safety of the products being manufactured and sold to Canadians and,
- processes to facilitate trade between Canada and other countries.

This is consistent with the mission of NHPD which is basically to ensure that all Canadians have ready access to natural health products that are safe, effective, and of high quality, while respecting freedom of choice and philosophical and cultural diversity.

In addition to the three phases of the research listed above, a consultation process was held on May 25, 2004 with the NHPD, Management Advisory Committee (MAC) of Health Canada. The MAC commented on a draft document entitled "International Regulation of Natural Health Products: Comparison of Natural Health Product Regulations for Canada's Primary Trading Partners." This comparison document consisted of the second phase of the research described above and it focussed on NHP Regulations for Canada's primary natural health product trading partners, namely, Australia, People's Republic of China, France, Germany, Hong Kong, India, United States, United Kingdom, and the European Union. The main purpose of the consultation process was to have an outside body, knowledgeable on the topic of international natural health product regulations, comment on the comparison phase of the research.

1.2   BACKGROUND AND HISTORY

Natural health products (NHPs) are big business both in Canada and elsewhere in the world. The majority of Canadian products previously registered as non-prescription medicines are now NHPs. Consumers are buying these products in record volumes all in an effort to make themselves feel better, get better, and to possibly live longer. The NHP industry shows no sign of fading. Currently poised above the billion-dollar mark in Canada alone, surveys reveal that more than 50% of Canadians are consuming NHPs. Estimates in the Unites States compiled by the Natural Foods Merchandiser put the sales of natural products and supplements in 2003 at more than $20.5 billion.

The term, natural health products, signals different things to different people. NHPs are common items, yet elusive in definition for the average Canadian. A glimpse at the large-scale nature of NHP choices is evident in terms of the reference used in the 1998 federal report *Natural Health Products: A New Vision*. This report identifies four major types of NHPs: traditional medicines including Chinese, Ayurvedic and North American Aboriginal medicines; traditional herbal medicines; homeopathic preparations; and vitamin and mineral supplements. Each of these types of NHPs represents an exhaustive line of products, offered in powders, tablets, oils, capsules, liquids, herbal teas, and other extracted forms.

In 2000, Health Canada's Office of Natural Health Products Transition Team worked diligently to define what they considered a natural health product. They described NHPs as composed of substances or combinations of substances found in nature, and energetically-potentized preparations, used for the purpose of maintaining or improving health or treating or preventing diseases or conditions. NHPs include, but are not limited to, the following classes of products: homeopathic preparations; vitamins; minerals; enzymes; coenzymes; co-factors; herbs or botanicals; naturally-occurring animal, plant and microorganism substances; and, a variety of molecules extracted from natural sources, such as amino acids, polysaccharides, peptides, naturally occurring hormones and biochemical intermediates, as well as naturally occurring molecules synthesized by chemical or biological means. It is NHP's health-enhancing potential that fuels the greatest interest.

In 1998, Health Canada began a process to examine the regulation of NHPs. A House of Commons Standing Committee on Health reviewed the regulations at that time and listened to the viewpoints of consumers, retailers, manufacturers, practitioners and others as to how these products should be regulated. Arising from this Committee was fifty-three recommendations that were accepted by Health Canada in 1999. A number of committee recommendations focused on research for NHPs. John Harrison, Manager, Office of Natural Health Products, Health Canada then, in 1999, held a research priority setting conference in Halifax, Nova Scotia. The recommendations from the participants of that conference were the following:

- that Health Canada immediately work with active researchers in the field to develop a strategy for achieving a Canadian Institute of Health Research (CIHR) for NHP research;
- that the research supported by Health Canada be of a initi-

ating nature, that it gives priority to cross-cutting research across disciplines, that it is delivered within a framework of an NHP research network and that research supported be relevant to industry and health care practitioners; and
- that the initial research supported relate to the creation of a credible database and to research into the safety, efficacy and standardization of existing NHPs.

Following this conference, Health Canada has had a number of focused consultations and commissioned a series of discussion papers related to policy, research and the regulatory aspects of NHPs. Topics included adverse reactions, current issues in Botanical Quality and quality controls and product standards. Further to these useful initiatives, there was a Natural Health Product Research Conference held between February 20th and 22nd, 2004 in Montreal, Quebec by the Natural Health Product Research Society of Canada. This conference connected NHP researchers with all interested stakeholders, government and funding partners. At this conference the global aspects of NHP research and regulations were discussed.

On January 1, 2004, Health Canada's new NHP Regulations came into force. These new regulations define NHPs for regulatory and legislative purposes as vitamins, minerals, herbs, homeopathic products, traditional medicines, probiotics, amino acids, essential fatty acids and extracts or isolates from plant and animal matter. These are the substances that will be legally considered NHPs.

The formal definition of included NHP substances is found in *Schedule 1 of the NHP Regulations* and this is:
1. A plant or a plant material, an alga, a bacterium, a fungus or a nonhuman animal matter.
2. An extract or isolate of a substance described in item 1, the primary molecular structure of which it had prior to its extraction or isolation.
3. Any of the following vitamins; biotin, folate, niacin, pantothenic acid, riboflavin, thiamine, vitamin A, vitamin B_6, vitamin B_{12}, vitamin C, vitamin D, vitamin E.
4. An amino acid.
5. An essential fatty acid.
6. A synthetic duplicate described in any of the items 2 to 5.
7. A mineral.
8. A probiotic.

The range of functions for which such products are used include the diagnosis, treatment, mitigation or prevention of a disease, disorder, or abnormal physical state or its symptoms in humans; restoring or correcting organic functions in humans; or modifying organic functions in humans, such as modifying those functions in a manner that maintains or promotes health.

Other governments have wrestled with defining NHPs. For instance, in 1994 the United States passed a *Dietary Supplement Health and Education Act (DSHEA)*, designed specifically to deal with dietary supplements. In the United States, homeopathic products are regulated under the *Food and Drug Act and Regulations* while in Canada this class of products is defined as a natural health product.

Canada's new regulatory framework is unique in the world and includes directives and guidelines for effective and informative labelling of products, requirements for site licences and product licences and standards of evidence that respect traditional evidence. The development of this framework involved an extensive series of consultations over a period of several years with consumers, practitioners, industry and all other relevant stakeholder groups. At these consultations consumers expressed their concerns which included the safety and toxicity of NHPs; and the need to ensure that what is advertized on the label is what is in the bottle in terms of product purity, potency and quality.

Health Canada's new NHP regulations came into effect in 2004. The major components of the Canadian regulatory framework for NHPs that were used for research comparison purposes were the following: Product Licensing including Standards of Evidence, Site Licensing, Good Manufacturing Practices and Adverse Reaction Reporting. Internationally, regulations and definitions of NHPs vary greatly from country to country. While on a national level regulations may address consumer needs, the lack of a mutually agreed legislative framework for the international scene can be a hindrance to international trade for these countries. Further, as consumers increasingly shop on-line, the laws and regulations in one country that are not rigorous can impact on the safety of consumers in another country.

Throughout the world there are problems associated with different regulatory requirements for NHPs. For example, in Europe, most natural health products such as homeopathic products are generally regulated as drugs. As a result, Canadian exporters of NHPs could have difficulty selling their products to Europe as drug regulations are generally perceived as more stringent than the *NHP Regulations*. For example, the Canadian good manufacturing practices for NHPs were not subject to the international mutual recognition agreements under which European NHPs are covered. This is an example of how differences in the regulation of these products can adversely affect Canadian trade with the world. Further, many of these regulations are quickly changing. Some of Canada's major trading partners in this NHP field are the United States, the United Kingdom, Europe, China, Australia and India. Many Canadian businesses import the raw materials from countries such as China and manufacture, formulate or repackage from these materials.

From a regulatory viewpoint, international legislation can come in many different forms including: enabling, prohibitive, restricting, quality control or monitoring based and/or those incorporating inspections, proof of efficacy and basic self-regulation. The menu of statutory instruments can include legislation, regulation, standards, guidelines and licences and foreign countries could have in their regulatory framework one or more of these instruments. One key issue is how NHPs are defined. For this project the Canadian definition of a natural health product is used as the standard to compare with for other countries.

CHAPTER 2

REVIEW OF THE RELATED
LITERATURE AND RESEARCH

This section describes the literature review on NHP Regulations and the legislative review for Canada's primary trading partners. The list of trading partners was based on a brief survey of trade volumes for each of the available and indicated NHPs.

2.1   LITERATURE REVIEW OF NATURAL HEALTH PRODUCT REGULATIONS FOR CANADA'S PRIMARY NHP TRADING PARTNERS

The literature review was based on examining various sources of literature including journals, books and internet searching. This literature review included a search by a commercial literature search agency NERAC (www.Nerac.com), accessed through a company. Documents were selected and ordered for review. Additional searches were conducted through internet search engines, "snowball" techniques where references in documents were accessed, and referrals from members of our professional networks. Searches were conducted in English, French, German and Mandarin, using combinations of key words as listed in the design chapter.

Most of the detailed documents are accessible from the internet and their internet addresses are listed. Some of the documents are very lengthy and detailed such as the paper on "Herbal medicinal products in the European Union" prepared by the Association of the European Self-Medication Industry. A second lengthy and useful document is the Harvard Law paper on DSHEA by S. Ray. For the purpose of this study, the papers, reports and documents considered to be most relevant and useful have been listed in the Reference List.

2.2 LEGISLATIVE REVIEW OF NATURAL HEALTH PRODUCT REGULATIONS FOR CANADA'S PRIMARY NHP TRADING PARTNERS

For the purpose of the legislative review of the NHP Regulations, pertinent information was obtained from the documents reviewed for the Literature Review part of the project. In addition the applicable Acts, Regulations and Directives were accessed for each of the countries surveyed. English texts were accessed for Australia, Canada, India, the United Kingdom, the United States and the European Union. Texts were accessed in French for the France's regulations, in German for Germany's regulations and in Mandarin for China's regulations. None of the German Acts and regulations were available in English and only a small part of the French and Chinese regulations were available in English. In addition , Codex Alimentarius documents were accessed as the results of the literature review suggested significant links between food, vitamin and mineral content and NHP's. The EU Directives on food and food supplements were reviewed for these same reasons.

Information from the literature review was separated into categories. These categories were definition, legislation/regulations/guidelines, regulatory agency, marketing authorization, product licencing/registration, risk/scientific assessments/standards of evidence, site licencing, good manufacturing practices and adverse reaction reporting. Information from each category for each country was then entered into Tables (1-22). Tables for the following countries were prepared; Australia, Canada, China, France, Germany, Hong Kong, India, United Kingdom and the United States along with Codex Alimentarius and the European Commission.

Appendix 1 lists the main web sites for the regulatory bodies covering NHPs in each country studied.

Generally, the information included in the tables showed that there are varied legislative regimes in the countries trading with Canada. However, the regulation regime of countries and future countries of the European Union will be streamlined into a common model based on the EU Directives that were initiated and approved since the first Directive was put into place in 1967. Notwithstanding this streamlining process, differences still exist in the interpretation of EU Directives, their implementation, and the "grandfathering" of different regulations that existed prior to the EU Directives (e.g. the German homeopathic regulations, the German and French drug laws). The EU regulates all European countries through Directives, forcing member states to adhere to common rules. The EU also considers most NHPs as drugs, but allows the member States some leeway in certain areas such as herbal products and homeopathics. The EU Directives set out prohibition versus strict adherence to required regulatory wording for the member states. Each individual member state in the EU has incorporated the appropriate EU Directives into their national laws and regulations. This has led to varying implementations. In the vitamins and minerals and the fortified food areas, the EU is inclusive in its regulations and this means that only what is included in the EU Directives is allowed in regulations of the member states. Further, in China there are differences in the standards applied to approved medications, and traditional medicines that are produced according to methods transferred in an oral tradition from generation to generation.

CHAPTER 3

DESIGN OF THE STUDY

3.1 LEGISLATIVE AND LITERATURE REVIEW

For the legislative review, information was collected from many sources including the internet sites for each country and their responsible departments, specialized internet sites, individuals and the scientific literature. In many cases the actual text of applicable Acts, Regulations and Directives were accessed at each country's web site and for the European Union (EU). Legislative documents were accessed in their original language (German, French, Mandarin) or in English where official translations existed.

Computer based literature searches were conducted using a variety of systems such as NERAC (nerac.com) and combinations of individual data bases such as Medline, CAB Health, Current Contents, the ERIC Database and Food Science and Technology Abstracts. In addition customized internet searches were conducted using tools such as the software "Copernic Meta", the "DogPile" and the Google search engines and Internet Explorer. A wide variety of search terms were used including the names of countries types of natural health products, coupled with the terms - international, comparison, herbal, botanical, review, regulatory, phytopharmaceutical, regulation, laws, codes, ordinances, guidelines and traditional.

3.2 CONSULTATION PROCESS WITH NHPD, MANAGEMENT ADVISORY COMMITTEE

On May 25, 2004, a presentation by John Harrison on the subject "International Regulation of Natural Health Products: Comparison of Natural Health Product Regulations for Canada's Primary Trading Partners" was given to the NHPD, MAC. From that presentation there was a discussion of this subject and the members of the committee were asked to provide written comments by June 5, 2004 to NHPD who, in turn, assembled the information and provided it to John Harrison. This information served as the main basis for this report along with the information from discussions held at that meeting. The MAC was also provided a copy of the Comparison document about a week before the May 25, 2004 meeting date so they could familiarize themselves with the document.

The following MAC committee members participated in the consultation; Yvan Bourgault (Canadian Homeopathic Pharmaceutical Association), Lawrence Cheng (Chamber of Chinese Herbal Medicine of Canada), Ron Dugas (La Societe du Langernate), Andre Gagnon (Natural Health Products Manufacturers of Canada), Albert Fok (Vancouver Chinatown Merchants Association), Connie Kehler (Saskatchewan Herb and Spice Association), Marie Provost (Guilde Des Herboristes La Clef des Champs Inc.), David Skinner (NDMAC), Paul Theriault (Direct Sellers Association of Canada) and Anne Wilkie (Canadian Health Food Association).

3.3 COMPARISON OF REGULATORY FRAMEWORKS

Information from each of the countries studied was compiled in comparison tables, and in extensive outlines of the legislative contents. From these compilations, an analysis comparing the Canadian regulatory framework with that of a number of countries was completed. The following specific regulatory areas were covered: definition of a natural health product, product licensing, standards of evidence, site licensing, good manufacturing practices, adverse reaction reporting and fortified foods. The following areas were discussed and analysed: level of regulation, standard of evidence, good manufacturing practices and good agricultural practices, adverse reaction reporting and trade with Canada. A set of eleven appendices outline the regulatory framework for each of the countries studied.

3.4 STRATEGY APPROACH FOR PRIORITIZED POLICY RESEARCH NEEDS

A list of strategies for the consideration of NHPD was prioritized based on their effectiveness and ease of implementation. The strategies covered trade considerations, trade strategies, safety strategies and mutual recognition agreements.

CHAPTER 4

RESULTS AND FINDINGS

4.1 LEGISLATIVE AND LITERATURE REVIEW

As a first step in this study a literature and legislative review was prepared on Natural Health Product Regulations for Canada's primary natural health products (NHP) trading partners, namely, Australia, China, France, Germany, Hong Kong, India, USA, United Kingdom, and the European Union. The Canadian NHP definition was used to compare similar classes of products for these other countries. Further, the major components of the Canadian regulatory framework for NHPs that were used for research purposes were the following: Product Licensing including Standards of Evidence, Site Licensing, Good Manufacturing Practices and Adverse Reaction Reporting.

Overall the more useful areas of the scientific literature in comparing international regulatory regimes for products such as herbal medicines, dietary supplements or homeopathic drugs were found on the web sites of international organizations such as the World Health Organization, the European Agency for the Evaluation of Medicinal Products and the Association of the European Self-Medication Industry. Another fruitful area was the Harvard Law papers prepared by Harvard undergraduates and graduates. There were only a limited number of scientific international regulatory comparison papers published in the open literature with the exception of World Health

Organization conference proceedings and other related clinical pharmacology conference proceedings. Most of the published scientific
papers are already outdated when published as the regulatory areas
of natural health products around the world are undergoing swift
changes. In addition, the actual (translated) texts of current Acts and
regulations were accessed to obtain relevant information.

Tables (1-22) were prepared for each country, providing sections
for certain aspects of the Canadian NHP regulatory framework and
including the main governmental regulatory authority for each country. Certain countries such as Australia have a regulatory regime very
comparable to Canada's while others such as China mainly export
only one type of NHP (e.g. Chinese herbal medicines). This is reflect-
ed in the type of Acts and Regulations each country has in force.

This review reveals a fast-paced change and revision of national
and international regulations for NHPs such as herbals, vitamins,
minerals and homeopathic medicines. Many changes in the European countries were precipitated by the implementation of European
Union Directives.

4.2   CONSULTATION PROCESS WITH NHPD, MANAGEMENT ADVISORY COMMITTEE

The presentation by John Harrison was well received by the MAC
members. Comments were solicited during and after the presentation and MAC members were invited to submit written comments.
MAC members present at the presentation either made comments
during the meeting or submitted comments after the meeting.

Many good comments were received from the Committee members and many of these comments were more future oriented and
strategic rather than reactive to the presentation of May 25, 2004.

It is important to point out that many of the suggestions made
and questions posed by the MAC fell into areas that were not directly within the terms of reference of the Comparison document
yet the suggestions and comments were pertinent and very useful
for possible future projects that could arise from the findings of the
Comparison document and become extensions of topics related to
this subject area.

The following points were raised by the Committee members:
- overall they wanted to know the regulatory and business
  trends that were occurring in the countries reviewed in the
  Comparison document;
- Italy was noted as having new regulations that address the

bulk herb situation and that NHPD might wish to examine these in more detail;

- for Canada and the other countries studied (with new regulations), they suggested it would be useful to know what the trends were in the NHP industry once new regulations came in and members asked if there were an increase in the number of companies or did the existing companies start selling more products or expanding a product base;
- why some countries were more stringent than others in terms of regulations;
- what was the impact of new regulations on the NHP industry in the countries reviewed and this comment was made in the context of increased regulations for industry;
- they brought up the subject of whether the existing regulations as well as emerging regulations had been included in the Comparison document and it was explained to them that, where possible, both aspects of regulations were included; the example was given of the Australian-New Zealand joint initiatives for complementary medicine regulations that had been included in the Comparison document, as well as the proposed EU regulations and Directives;
- the subject of Canada's Bill C-420 that had been considered by the last Parliament was discussed and the recent testimony of Dr. Phil Waddington to the House of Commons Standing Committee on Health was mentioned;
- Japan, a country not included in the Comparison document, has deregulated this area of NHPs to some extent;
- it was suggested that Mexico, Brazil and Japan be further studied as Mexico is part of NAFTA, Brazil produces various NHPs and Japan is deregulating this NHP area.

4.3   COMPARISON OF REGULATORY FRAMEWORKS

In preparing the comparison of regulations and legislation for NHPs in Canada to those of Canada's main trading partners, the framework of the Canadian legislation was used as the starting point. The Canadian NHP Regulations were separated into the following components:

- definition of natural health products,
- product licensing,
- standards of evidence,
- site licensing,

- good manufacturing practices/good agricultural practices
- adverse reaction reporting, and
- fortified foods and their regulation.

For each of these topics, the Canadian example was used as a basis for comparison. For each of the main trading partners, information was briefly described in the comparison, and the details were placed in Appendices 2-12.

4.3.1 DEFINITION OF A NATURAL HEALTH PRODUCT

This section addresses the definition of an NHP in Canada and provides the comparison of the Canadian definition with that of Canada's main trading partners. Definitions are varied in different countries and include or exclude certain classes of products.

Canadian Situation

The NHP definition in Canada has two components: function and substance. The function component refers to the natural health product definition capturing those substances that are manufactured, sold or represented for use in:

- the diagnosis, treatment, mitigation of prevention of a disease, disorder or abnormal physical state or its symptoms in humans;
- restoring or correcting organic functions in humans; or
- modifying organic functions in humans, such as modifying those functions in a manner that maintains or promotes health.

The substance component refers to the medicinal ingredient in a natural health product. These substances include, but are not limited to, traditional herbal medicines, traditional Chinese herbal remedies, Ayurvedic and Native North American medicines, homeopathic medicines, vitamins and mineral supplements, probiotics and essential fatty acids.

Included NHP substances are listed in *Schedule 1 of the NHP Regulations*:

1. A plant or a plant material, an alga, a bacterium, a fungus or a nonhuman animal matter.
2. An extract or isolate of a substance described in item 1, the primary molecular structure of which it had prior to its extraction or isolation.

3. Any of the following vitamins; biotin, folate, niacin, pantothenic acid, riboflavin, thiamine, vitamin A, vitamin B_6, vitamin B_{12}, vitamin C, vitamin D, vitamin E.
4. An amino acid.
5. An essential fatty acid.
6. A synthetic duplicate described in any of the items 2 to 5.
7. A mineral.
8. A probiotic.

International Comparison

The Canadian definition was compared with those of Canada's main trading partners. On the whole, the definitions deal with the functionality of the NHPs, where the substance in certain cases modifies the conditions required under the functionality. For several trading partners, all NHPs fall under the concept of "drug" or "medicine." This is the case for the European Union (EU) and therefore generally covers Germany, France and the United Kingdom. As the EU allows member states to modify the requirements under the EU Directives based on prior regulations, certain substances have been integrated in the member state's regulations. This is particularly true for homeopathic medicine in Germany and France, and herbal medicine in Germany, China and India use the functionality principle and classify NHPs as drugs or food. However, China also recognizes Traditional Chinese Medicine, and health food products as separate substance classes. The United States and Australia base their definitions on substances and their workings, over functionality.

Australia defines *complementary medicine* (CM) as a therapeutic good consisting wholly or principally of one or more designated active ingredients, each of which has a clearly established identity and a traditional use; these include herbal medicines, homeopathic medicines, vitamins and mineral supplements, traditional medicines such as Ayurvedic medicines, traditional Chinese medicines, other nutritional supplements, and aromatherapy oils. Traditional use means use of the well documented and designated active ingredient according to the accumulated experience of traditional healthcare practitioners.

China defines the NHPs in three categories: Drugs are articles that are used in the prevention, treatment and diagnosis of human diseases and intended for the regulation of the physiological functions of human beings, for which indications, usage and dosage are established, including Chinese crude drugs, prepared slices of crude drugs, traditional Chinese medicines preparations, chemical drug substances and their preparations, antibiotics, biochemical drugs, radioactive pharmaceuticals, serum, vaccines, blood products and diagnostic tests. China also recognizes a class of substances as Traditional Chinese Medicine (TCM). TCM includes Chinese Medicinal Herbs (Dan Fang) and Chinese Prepared Medicines (Cheng Fang). TCM is recorded in the Pharmacopoeia of the People's Republic of China (PRC). There are more than eighteen defined categories of Single Herbs and eighteen defined categories of Herbal Formulas in TCM herbal medicine. China also recognizes a class of health food products, any food product that has been tested and scientifically proven to have unmistakable and reliable health benefits and no acute, malignant, or chronic damaging effects to the human body.

The **European Union** is precise in its description of NHPs. The EU includes all NHPs under the concept of medical products. The EU defines *medical products* as any substance or combination of substances which may be administered to human beings to make a medical diagnosis or to restore, correct or modify physiological functions in humans.

Substance is defined as any matter of the following origin: human, animal (including microorganisms, organs, secretions, parts, extractions), vegetable (including microorganisms, plants, plant parts, extracts, secretions) and chemical. Within this definition of medical products, medical strength vitamins and minerals are included. However, for food supplements, supplements that are prepackaged and marked as foods and in concentrated form to supplement the normal diet and having nutritional and physiological effects (e.g., vitamins and minerals) are under a different EU Directive. *Homeopathic medicines* are defined as any product made from products, substances and compositions called source substances, through a homeopathic manufacturing process described in the European pharmacopoeia, the French pharmacopoeia or, if not available, in the pharmacopoeia officially utilized in another member state of the European Community.

In **Germany** all NHPs fall under the definition of Arzneimittel or *drugs*: All substances designed to treat, heal, sooth or prevent disease or injury in humans and animals. Homeopathic medicine is defined as all medicine registered in the Homeopathic Medicine Register. *Plant-based products labelled with the German common name* are in a special class and have a marketing authorization different from drugs, but are still defined as drugs.

Hong Kong has two categories of NHPs in two classifications: The first category includes Chinese Herbal medicine (Herbs) which are defined by two herbal schedules; one for potent herbs sold through prescription use only, and another that lists 574 commonly used herbs that are sold without prescription; the second category is Proprietary Chinese Medicine that includes and proprietary product composed solely of the following as active ingredients: (I) any Chinese herbal medicine; or (ii) any materials of herbal, animal or mineral origin customarily used by the Chinese; or any medicines and materials referred to in (I) or (ii). Both categories comprise products that are formulated in a finished dose form and known or claimed to be used for the diagnosis, treatment, prevention or alleviation of any disease or any symptom of a disease in human beings, or for the regulation of the functional states of the human body.

India classifies NHPs as either drugs or foods. The *drug* category includes herbal medicine, Ayurvedic medicine, homeopathic medicine, and those food supplements considered medicine. Food supplements not considered medicine are defined as foods.

The **United Kingdom** defines NHPs either as drugs or as foods. Within the drug category are *Herbal Products* which as defined as a medicinal product consisting of a substance produced by subjecting a plant or plants to drying, crushing or any other process, or of a mixture whose sole ingredients are two or more substances so produced, or of a mixture whose sole ingredients are one or more substances so produced and water or some other inert substance. Also included are *homeopathic medicines* defined as any medicinal product prepared from products, substances or composition called homeopathic stocks in accordance with a homeopathic manufacturing procedure described by the European pharmacopoeia or, in the absence thereof, by the pharmacopoeias currently used officially by the member states (e.g., EU definition in use), and food supplements are defined as supplements for which medicinal claims are made (e.g., to treat, prevent or cure) or which are administered to restore, correct or modify physiological function. Vitamins and minerals without medical claims are considered food.

In the **USA** some NHPs are classified as *dietary supplements*: a product taken by mouth that contains a "dietary ingredient" (DI) intended to supplement the diet. The DIs in these products may include herbs or other botanicals, vitamins, minerals, amino acids or a dietary substance for use by humans to supplement the diet by increasing the total dietary intake; or a concentrate, metabolite, constituent, extract or combination of any of the above ingredients. The USA also defines "New Dietary Ingredients" as products where pre-market review for safety data and other information is required by law. DSHEA restricts nutritional support claims made on dietary supplement (DS) labels to descriptions of the "role of a nutrient or dietary ingredient intended to affect the structure or function in humans" or "the documented mechanism by which the supplement acts to maintain such structure or function." A Food and Drug Act (FDA) disclaimer is required on DS, stating that the FDA has not evaluated it and the product is not intended to diagnose, treat, cure, or prevent any disease. Homeopathic medicines are defined as articles listed in the Homeopathic Pharmacopoeia of the United States and are legally defined as *drugs*. Other NHPs are classified as nonprescription medicine and are regulated under the authority of the FDA.

4.3.2 PRODUCT LICENSING

Products are required to be licensed before they can be put on the market. The licensing process includes a review of all available data on safety testing, efficacy testing and in some cases production processes. This review leads to the issuing of a product licence. Products can be licensed individually on a risk-based evaluation, or no licence could be required.

Canadian Situation

Part 1 (Product Licences) of the *Natural Health Products Regulations* sets out requirements for product licensing and the responsibilities of the product licence holder. The *NHP Regulations* require an individual to obtain a product licence prior to selling an NHP in Canada. The following guidance documents set out more information:
- Product Licensing Guidance Document,
- Evidence for Quality of Finished Natural Health Products,
- Evidence for Safety and Efficacy of Finished Natural Health Products,
- List of Acceptable Non-medicinal Ingredients,
- Compendium of Monographs,
- Homeopathics Guidance Document,
- The Adverse Reaction Reporting Guidance Document-For Health Care Providers and Consumers.

International Comparison

A review of the regulations for Canada's main trading partners reveals that Canada's licensing and registration requirements are comparable with the licensing requirements of the EU and EU member states. The EU requires licensing of all NHPs using a guidance document or monograph, including information on manufacturing, marketing, labelling requirements, responsibility for products, products quality, etc. India requires registration and licensing of all NHPs and China and Hong Kong requires registration and licensing of products classified as drugs. Australia requires registration of high risk NHPs and listing of low risk NHPs, while the USA requires neither licensing nor registration of "current" NHPs. In the USA new dietary substances require a pre-market safety review, which is considered licensing although this route is rarely taken. Other U.S. NHPs just require notification. Details for each of Canada's main trading partners follow.

Australia: The Therapeutic Goods Administration (TGA) maintains the Australian Register of Therapeutic Goods (ARTG). Complementary Medicines (CMs) may be included on the ARTG as Listed (lower risk) or as Registered Medicines (higher risk). Listed Medicines (LM) carry the designation AUST R and a unique number and may be OTC or available by prescription from a medical doctor or authorized prescriber. Both Australia's licensing and evaluation systems are risk based.

In Australia, registration is a more detailed process than listing and requires pre-market evidence of safety and efficacy. Indications and claims for LMs are not subject to pre-market evaluation (e.g., health maintenance, health enhancement). The indications and claims for Registered Medicines relate to treatment, management, and cure of disease and disorders.

China: For health food products licensing is not mentioned, but the product is required to have claims verified and registered with the Ministry of Health. Drugs are licensed by the Centre for Drug Evaluation. TCM licensing is mentioned in short summaries of regulatory documents. It is included in the Regulation 61 (Directive Guo Ban Fa 2002). This Directive outlines the strategic goals for modernizing TCM, highlighting the guiding philosophy, fundamental principles, important projects and measures to be taken to attain those goals. There are provisions for two types (class 1 and class 2) of TCM Varieties Protection. Class 1 products have special efficacy in treating diseases, are made from class 1 Wild Herbal Medicine Materials and can prevent and treat a specific disease. Class 2 products either meet the class 1 criteria or have marked efficacy in treating specific diseases and are made from the active ingredients of special formulations from natural medicines. Their TCM regulations are also differentiated into those for packaged and prepared TCM and each have specific packaging and marketing regulations(Guo Shi Yao Jian Ban (2003) 358). The package material and containers of prepared TCM should not affect the quality of the prepared TCM. The prepared TCM products should be labelled with commodity name, specification, place and date of production, batch number and licence number if available. The prepared TCM products should be properly packaged for the transportation process and products not in conformance with the regulations should not be marketed. Order 374, 2003 describes professionals, education and research and health care measures. Order 106, 1992 classifies the TCM products.

EU: All products need to be licenced. Licensing takes place through the member states, or for specific cases through the EU. Licensing is based on the review of documentation specifically outlined in the EU Directives.

France: All products must be registered with the French Agency for the Safety of Medical Products. Food supplements and vitamins are required to be registered to conform with the EU Directives.

Germany: All products require licensing. Licensing is based on a review of documentation by Commissions (Commission E for herbal products, Commission C for anthroposophic products and Commission D for homeopathic medicine).

Hong Kong requires registration of Proprietary Chinese Medicine only, for the categories of well-established drugs, new drugs and health products.

India: All products require registration and licensing under the *Drugs and Cosmetics Act*.

United Kingdom: All industrially manufactured products need to be registered and licensed. Vitamins, food supplements at medical strength, and homeopathics are registered and licensed under EU Directives.

USA: "Current" dietary supplements do not need review or approval from the FDA and are not licensed. No claims can be made for these products. New Dietary ingredients are required to submit a pre-market safety review. Homeopathic medicines are listed in the Homeopathic Pharmacopoeia and only those listed are recognized.

4.3.3 STANDARDS OF EVIDENCE

The Standards of Evidence (SOE) framework consists of clearly defined criteria concerning the amount and type of evidence required to support each product claim for safety, efficacy and quality. For a health related claim to be allowed it must correspond to the level and totality of the evidence of efficacy available. Evaluating the safety of natural health products can consist of an analysis for the full range of efficacy, toxicological and safety data. All this data often does not exist and different types of evidence must be recognized in the SOE process. For example, if the history of use for the product is available, this may be used. Quality is a key issue for consumers. Quality may be defined as the integration of the many variable characteristics and properties that may significantly affect product efficacy and product safety. Product quality assurance could be considered the process by which the product manufacturer ensures that potential variations in raw materials, processed and finished products remain within acceptable limits. Overall safety is the main factor. If the SOE for quality is not adequate, it does not mean the product will be banned whereas if the evidence for safety is inadequate then the product will be banned or severely restricted.

Many adverse effects from NHPs have been traced to quality control programs such as contamination. To counter this problem, manufacturers, importers, packagers and labellers of NHPs will be required to submit evidence of compliance to NHP good manufacturing practices (GMPs) to obtain a site licence. General specifications include tolerance limits for contaminants, while specifications unique to a specific substance may include chemical tests for markers to identify a particular plant species or variety of a herb, or for levels of active or toxic constituents to support specific safety and efficacy claims.

Canadian Situation

Canada's SOE approach for natural health products recognizes that a gradient of evidence strength exists and varying strengths of evidence can be used to support the claims of safety and efficacy in a product licence application. All full product licence applications for Canadian NHPs must contain a "safety summary report" highlighting any safety issues identified in a thorough review of published scientific literature. For products that have never been used in humans, repeat-dose toxicity, genotoxicity and reproductive toxicology testing will be required.

In Canada, products are divided into two categories according to the claim:

- traditional use claims
- non-traditional use claims.
- Types of claims are the following:
- treatment claims relate to the diagnosis, treatment and mitigation or prevention of disease, disorder, or an abnormal physical state or its symptoms in humans;
- risk reduction claims describe the relationship between using a medicinal ingredient and reducing risk of developing a specific disease or abnormal physiological state, by significantly altering a major risk factor or factors recognized to be involved in the development of the chronic disease or abnormal physiological state; and
- structure function claims describe the effect of a medicinal ingredient on a structure or physiological function in the body, or a medicinal ingredient's support of an anatomical, physiological, or mental function.

In general, the types of evidence to support the claims and their conditions of use can be categorized into the following:

- references to traditional use;
- references to scientific evidence;
- references from Expert Opinion Reports;
- references from reputable regulatory authority reports; and
- references to previous marketing experience.

The applicant may use any of the above types of evidence listed as long as the evidence is sufficient to support the type of claim being made (i.e., for a traditional use claim the applicant must submit two independent references that support the traditional use and the conditions of use and show fifty years of consecutive use). The guidance documents that are applicable to this area of Standards of Evidence include Evidence of Safety, Evidence of Finished NHPs and Evidence for Quality of Finished NHPs.

International Comparison

All of Canada's main trading partners require standards of evidence to make sure that any substance is safe for use as a self care product. In most countries this is the same standard of evidence used for drugs or medicinal products. The USA classifies some NHPs as dietary substances and they do not require proof of evidence for such products. Other NHPs must submit a drug application to the FDA or notify the FDA of the sale of a monographed NHP. New products in the USA that are not considered drugs may be screened by lower standards or not at all, or with unclear standards. The standards of evidence for homeopathic medicines can be different for some of Canada's main trading partners.

Australia

Listed Medicines (LM) evaluation uses a process that aims to ensure any substance approved for use is of low risk. Four types of data are used to support safety evaluation in LMs: biological activity, toxicology, clinical trials and adverse reactions. Registered Medicines (RM) evaluation uses standards of quality, safety and efficacy as required for self-care and prescription products.

For identified risks or potential health risks from an LM or RM, restrictions may be imposed such as label advisory information, dosage restrictions, route of administration or plant part and/or restriction of the form in which the substance can be used.

China

This country has a standards of evidence framework. These standards are only implemented for drugs and health food products. The standards for Traditional Herbal Medicine are unclear, and appear to be based on local folklore, local agricultural practices and plant growing methods.

EU

The standards of evidence for herbals and homeopathic medicines are described in the EU Directives and are enforced through the member states. Some reduced requirements exist for herbal products and homeopathic products.

France

Vitamins that qualify as drugs, food supplements and homeopathic drugs require rigorous standards of evidence. Herbal products do not require the same standards of evidence.

Germany

Natural health products are assessed by the respective Commissions according to rigorous standards of evidence.

Hong Kong

Hong Kong uses two schedules for Chinese Herbal Medicine: one for potent herbs and a second for 574 commonly used herbs. Prescriptions are prepared by Chinese medicine practitioners for potent herbs. Products can make claims to have general beneficial effects on health. The registration system is based on safety, quality and efficacy.

For Proprietary Chinese Medicine, claims can be made to prevent or cure a specific disease or clinical condition substantiated with a clinical trial and medicinal test results.

India

All NHPs are regulated under the evidence requirements of the *Drug and Cosmetics Act*.

United Kingdom

Standards of evidence exist for all NHPs classified as medical products. Non-medical products such as some vitamins and some food supplements are exempt.

USA

A dietary supplement (DS) manufacturer is responsible for ensuring that a DS is safe before it is marketed. The U.S. Food and Drug Administration is responsible for taking action against any unsafe DS product after it is on the market. DSHEA lists four reasons that a DS could be adulterated making it subject to FDA regulation. These reasons are: the DS poses a "significant or unreasonable risk of illness or injury" when used according to label directions; the DS contains a new ingredient that cannot be shown to be safe; the Secretary declares the DS poses an "imminent hazard to public health or safety"; or the DS contains "poisonous or unsanitary" ingredients pursuant to the Federal Food, Drug and Cosmetic Act (FDC Act).

The *FDC Act* is the responsible act for defining a homeopathic drug. When the *FDC Act* was passed in 1938, homeopathic products were essentially grand-fathered into the definition of a drug. Manufacturers of homeopathic products are required to register their premises as drug establishments in conformance with Section 510 of the *FDC Act* and Code of Federal Regulations 207. Depending on label claims, these products are sold as OTCs or prescription products.

4.3.4 SITE LICENSING

Requirements for site licensing include obtaining approval for a manufacturing or distribution site. Site licensing allows for the safeguarding of proper procedures in manufacturing and distribution.

Canadian Situation

Part 2 of the Natural Health Product Regulations sets out the requirements for site licensing and the responsibilities of a site licence holder. A site licence, in accordance with the Good Manufacturing Practices (GMPs), is required for manufacturers, packagers, labellers and importers of natural health products. The product license application must also include similar information with respect to all foreign sites performing any regulated activities. A Site Licence Guidance Document is available on the NHPD website: *www.hc-sc.gc.ca/hpfb-dgpsa/nhpd-dpsn.*

International Comparison

Most of Canada's main trading partners in NHPs require site licensing as the products are considered to be drugs or medicine. The EU and its member states require site licensing procedures for all products, as do Australia, Hong Kong and India. Some of Canada's main trading partners do not require site licensing for vitamins and minerals as long as they are not classified as drugs or medicine. In China, "drugs" require a site licence, while the "health food products" and "Traditional Chinese Medicine" do not require a site licence. In the USA, the NHPs that are considered dietary supplements do not require site licensing while those that are not dietary supplements do require site licensing. Manufacturers of homeopathic products in the USA are required to register their premises as drug establishments.

Australia

Australian manufacturers of medicinal products for human use must hold a manufacturing licence. It is an offence, carrying heavy penalties, to manufacture therapeutic goods without such a licence, unless the goods are exempt from this requirement. Licence holders are required to comply with the manufacturing principles of the *Therapeutic Goods Act*. These principles require compliance with the Good Manufacturing Practice.

China

Site licensing exists for "drugs" as there are Good Manufacturing Practices in place. No evidence was found for site licensing of health food products or Traditional Chinese Medicine products.

EU

Based on EU Directives, all EU member countries are required to provide for site licensing of medical products.

France
Site licensing is required for all medical products, including herbs and vitamins, and homeopathic medicines. Site licensing is accomplished through the French Food Safety Agency or the European Agency for the Evaluation of Medicinal Products (EMEA). Non-medicinal food products must adhere to the French Food Laws.

Germany
Site licensing is required for all medical products including herbs and vitamins, and homeopathic medicine. Site licensing is by the local governments (Lander), rather than the federal authority.

Hong Kong
Site licensing is in place for importers, manufacturers and retailers.

India
Herbal products, food supplements and homeopathic medicines have site licensing arrangements under the *Drug and Cosmetic Act*. There is no indication that vitamins and minerals are covered.

United Kingdom
Manufacturers of herbal products and homeopathic medicines require a Manufacturer's licence. Manufacturers of vitamins and minerals only need a Manufacturer's licence if the products are classified as medicines.

USA
There is no site licence requirement for dietary substances. However, there are site licence requirements for other NHPs such as homeopathic products.

4.3.5   GOOD MANUFACTURING PRACTICES

Worldwide, medicinal plants are mostly collected in the wild. The rapid growth of the herbal NHP industry has led to over-harvesting of certain plants according to a World Wildlife Federation (WWF) study. Few companies show real concern regarding the ecological and social sustainability of harvesting practices. NHPs for a large part are plant, animal, bacteria, fungi and algae based and are prepared from materials grown in the laboratory or in nature. Specifically, plant materials grown outdoors could be susceptible to contamination from fertilizer materials, environmental factors or human pathogenic micro-organisms. In case of wild-crafted plants from the un-amended natural soil, the uncontrolled and unmonitored status of the natural soil may affect the quality of the harvested materials.

Environmental vectors could affect plants used to prepare herbal

NHPs during growth from residues in the soil, irrigation water, fertilizer and specific plant protection products. Microbial contamination could take place during growth when (organic) fertilizer materials are used, during harvesting and during processing. Procedures must be put in place to prevent the contamination of herbal NHPs with undesirable compounds and pathogens. Strict, monitored methods for production and handling of plant and other materials during the growing process and the processing are required to protect the NHPs. Currently, programs of voluntary guidelines, monitoring and assessment have been developed in many countries. Such programs for agricultural production are called Good Agricultural Practices (GAP). Similar programs have been developed for work in laboratories (Good Laboratory Practices, GLPs) and manufacturing (Good Manufacturing Practices, GMP). These programs when implemented in a company or production facility are verified by an external body. For instance, for GLPs two main bodies verify and accredit laboratories: the OECD and the United States Environmental Protection Agency. Procedures to be followed and their verification methods are very similar.

Several jurisdictions have developed GAP and are verifying and accrediting these GAPs. GAP programs are often geared toward a specific goal. For instance, the GAPs in England and Ireland are targeting environmental effects of farming on soil, water and air. Through following of a GAP process, farmers protect the environment and reduce their liability and consumers of products are ensured of a standard quality. In the U.S. and Europe, GAPs have been developed and are implemented to protect food from microbial contamination. The United States Department of Agriculture manages a nation wide program for GAP to prevent microbial contamination in fresh fruits and vegetables. This program called the Federal-State Inspection Service Audit Verification Program was developed and administered by Cornell University through the Good Agricultural Practices project and has the cooperation of the U.S. FDA and operates in several States. The program provides audits and posts audit results on a website and approved facilities receive a certificate.

The Eurep program (see: *http://www.eurep.org/*)of GAP sets the minimum standards for leading retail groups in Europe for the production of horticultural products (e.g., fruits, vegetables, potatoes, etc.). Eurep is an initiative of retailers belonging to the Euro-Retailer Produce Working Group. It has subsequently evolved into an equal partnership of agricultural producers and their retail customers. Its mission is to develop widely accepted standards and procedures for the global certification of Good Agricultural Practices. Independent verification takes place by an Eurep approved body. GAPs include the Integrated Pest Management and Integrated Crop Management. Independent verification takes place by a Eurep approved body.

Good Agricultural Practices are focussed on the product and specific aspects of the production process, while other (voluntary) programs such as ISO 9000 and 9002, and ISO 14000 for manufacturing and environmental practices respectively, as well as the ISO 65 for certified organic production are focussed on the flow of information in a facility.

Canadian Situation

Part 3 of the *Natural Health Product Regulations* sets out the requirements for meeting good manufacturing practices - measures designed to ensure an effective overall approach to product quality control and risk management. They do so by setting appropriate standards and practices for product testing, manufacturing, storage, handling and distribution. The Good Manufacturing Practices Guidance Document outlines in detail the requirements for the manufacturing, packaging, labelling, importing and distributing of natural health products.

International Comparison

All of Canada's main trading partners require that manufacturers of drugs or medicines follow GMP practices. For dietary supplements (DS), the USA currently requires GMPs applicable to food products. However the U.S. has recently proposed GMPs specific to DS and for the other NHPs, the drug GMPs apply. Hong Kong requires the production of herbal products according to GMPs and Good Agricultural Practices. The PRC requires for all NHPs a Good Management Practice, Good Laboratory Practices, Good Clinical Practice, and Good Agricultural Practices (GAP). For Traditional Chinese Medicine, GAPs are required to be met for plants and animals.

Australia

Manufacturers of medicinal products for human use must hold a manufacturing licence. It is an offence, carrying heavy penalties, to manufacture therapeutic goods without such a licence, unless the goods are exempt from this requirement. In 2003 there was a regulatory tightening up of this area. Licence holders are required to comply with the manufacturing principles of the *Therapeutic Goods Act.*

These principles require compliance with the Australian Code for Good Manufacturing Practice (GMP).

China

Drugs are manufactured according to GMPs. Herbal products, Traditional Chinese Medicine products and Chinese Crude Drugs are produced according to GMPs and Good Agricultural Practices. Traditional Chinese Medicine products are produced according to GAPs for Traditional Medicine Plants and Animals. In addition, PRC adheres to a "Green Code" describing the use/harvest of wild crafted products.

EU

Several EU Directives, including 91/356/EEC require GMPs. Manufacturing practices must be described in the documents to be submitted for a site licence or marketing authorization, and are thus approved by the Regulators in member states.

France

Following EU Directive 91/356/EEC and others, France requires that manufacturers follow GMP programs.

Germany

Following EU Directive 91/356/EEC and others, Germany requires that manufacturers follow GMP programs.

Hong Kong

Manufacturers are required to follow the GMPs for the two classes of NHPs (Chinese Herbal Medicine and Proprietary Chinese Medicine) in Hong Kong. Hong Kong also requires production of plant and animal products according to Good Agricultural Practices.

India

GMP Standards of the Ayurvedic and Unani pharmacopoeias are to be followed. Manufacturers must also follow Good Manufacturing Practices as per Schedule M of the *Drugs and Cosmetics Act*. GMP Standards provided in the homeopathic pharmacopoeia are to be followed.

United Kingdom

The United Kingdom is covered by the EU Directive 91/356/EEC and others. Industrially produced herbal medicinal products and homeopathic products are subject to the same good manufacturing practices as all other medicinal products. Exempt herbal remedies are not covered by the GMP regulations. Vitamins and minerals must be prepared and packaged in accordance with the *Food Supplements Regulations (England)*.

USA

DS products are required to be prepared, packaged, and stored in accordance with current good manufacturing practices applicable to food products. All ingredients must be truthfully and accurately listed on the label and the product may not be adulterated with other substances.

The FDA has recently proposed (May 6, 2003) DS regulations in current good manufacturing practices. These will not impose standards for which there is no current and generally available analytical methodology. There are drug GMPs in place for other non-prescription products.

4.3.6 ADVERSE REACTION REPORTING

Adverse reaction reporting provides a mechanism to collect data on adverse patient reaction, and allows the Regulators to implement measures to protect the public. Adverse reaction reporting can be achieved on a voluntary or regulated basis.

Canadian Situation

Within Part 1 (Product Licensing) of the *Natural Health Product Regulations*, Section 24 sets out the regulations for Reaction Reporting. A licensee has to produce a) a case report for each serious adverse reaction to the natural health product that occurs inside Canada, within 15 days of becoming aware of it and b) a case report for each serious unexpected adverse reaction to the natural health product that occurs inside or outside of Canada, within 15 days of becoming aware of it.

International Comparison

The adverse reaction reporting for NHPs in Canada's main trading partners varies from full reporting for all drugs, homeopathic medicine, and vitamins and minerals, (e.g., European Countries and EC Directive; China), to voluntary reporting requirements (e.g., Australia, USA) and no requirements (e.g., India).

Australia

Monitoring of adverse reactions to Complementary Medicines (CMs) is conducted using a Blue Card System that is a voluntary reporting system; Sponsors of all medicines in the ARTG are under an obligation to report adverse reactions to the TGA. These reports are entered into the Adverse Drug Reaction Reporting System database. Serious reaction reports are reviewed by TGA MD and are also reviewed by the Adverse Drug Reaction Advisory Committee. Summary reports for CMs are also sent to the Complementary Medicines Evaluation Committee for advice.

China

Adverse drug reaction reporting procedures are in place for Drugs and for Health food products, and are reported to be in place for Traditional Chinese Medicine.

EU

Adverse drug reaction reporting procedures are in place for herbal products, vitamins and minerals and homeopathic products. Reporting procedures on food supplements are unclear.

France

Adverse drug reaction reporting procedures are in place for all NHP products classified as drugs.

Germany

Adverse drug reaction reporting procedures are in place for all NHP products classified as drugs.

Hong Kong

Guidelines for adverse drug reaction reporting are under development.

India

No system for adverse drug reaction reporting is in place in India.

United Kingdom

Adverse drug reaction reporting is required for herbal and homeopathic products, except for vitamins and minerals or food supplements.

USA

Reporting adverse reactions is voluntary and carries no legal obligations. The FDA enters and analyses all reports of adverse events they receive into the Center for Food Safety and Applied Nutrition's Special Nutritionals Adverse Event Monitoring System. The FDA also uses its MedWatch system to track serious events. The FDA receives passive surveillance data on adverse events associated with food and dietary supplements through the Drug Quality Reporting System and the Office of Regulatory Affairs Consumer Complaint System.

4.3.7   FORTIFIED FOODS

Fortified foods are foods that have vitamins, minerals and other substances added to either replace ingredients lost in processing, to add to the food to increase its benefits, or to provide other characteristics. Currently large shifts in regulation are taking place in the area of fortified foods, and foods in general, as this is an area of market development. Most regulations are still in the design or consultation stage. This section describes the situation as of January, 2004.

Canadian Situation

Fortification is the addition of essential nutrients, especially vitamins and minerals, at levels above those normally found in the particular type of food to which they have been added to address a deficiency or inadequate intake of the nutrient in the diet of people. Vitamins and minerals may also be added to restore those lost due to food processing, to make a substitute food nutritionally equivalent to the food for which it is substituting, or to make a special purpose food, including sole sources of nutrition.

In Canada the legislation for the addition of vitamins and minerals to ordinary foods is of the "General Permission" type. General Permission refers to the situation where nutrient addition is regulated by legislation, which specifies the foods and /or nutrients permitted and also the levels of the nutrients which might be permitted. In Canada's case, the allowed nutrients and their levels are specified in foods. The addition of vitamins and minerals (micronutrients) to foods in Canada is controlled under regulatory provisions first promulgated in 1964 (Part D, Division 3, Food and Drug Regulations). The Food and Drug Regulations specify the foods to which micronutrients may be added, the micronutrients and the levels to which they may be added to these foods. The regulations state the amount of nutrient that must be present in the food at the time of purchase. To add to the list of foods that may contain added micronutrients or to the list of nutrients, an amendment is required to the Food and Drug Regulations. The criteria for determining the acceptability of a nutrient addition to a food are based on the Guidelines for the Addition of Nutrients to Foods (Trade Information Letter Number 351) and the General Principles for the Addition of Essential Nutrients to Foods established by the Codex Alimentarius Commission.

The Canadian Parliamentary Bill C-420 was in second reading in March, 2005 and, if passed, this Bill would classify the Natural Health Products Regulations as subset of the food regulations. Therefore, it was thought useful to briefly discuss the area of fortified foods. Bill C-420 would define "food" as any article grown, manufactured, sold or represented for use as food or drink for human beings, chewing gum, and any ingredient that may be mixed with food for any purpose whatever, including dietary supplements, herbs and other natural health products.

International Comparison

Of Canada's trading partners, only the USA and Germany have established regulations for fortified foods. Germany establishes which additives (vitamins and minerals) can be included and how much. The USA requires a pre-market approval of food additives, and Australia only allows vitamins and minerals in foods that conform to their standards. Several international bodies including the EC and the Codex Alimentarius are drafting regulations regarding the inclusion of vitamins and minerals (and other substances) in foods. None of these processes is complete, but when complete the regulations and Directives will affect Canada's trading partners in Europe (EC Directives), Canada's trading partners in Europe and outside Europe and Canada itself may be affected by the Codex Alimentarius should these countries ratify the Codex.

Australia/New Zealand

Australia and New Zealand have developed a partnership with eight other governments in the region to form the Food Standards Australia New Zealand. This body is responsible for developing, varying and reviewing standards and codes of conduct with industry for food available in Australia and New Zealand covering labelling, composition and contaminants. The standards include an inclusive regulation on vitamins and minerals, which are only allowed when expressly mentioned in the Standard.

Codex Alimentarius

The Codex Alimentarius Commission or Codex was created in 1963 by Food and Agriculture Organization of the United Nations (FAO) and World Health Organization to develop food standards, guidelines and related texts such as codes of practice. The Codex defines several substances. For the purpose of the Codex "Guidelines for Vitamins and Mineral Food Supplements," vitamin and mineral food supplements are defined as deriving their nutritional relevance primarily from the minerals and /or vitamins they contain. Vitamin and mineral supplements are sources in concentrated forms of those nutrients alone or in combination, marketed in forms such as capsules, tablets, powders, solutions, etc., not in conventional food form and whose purpose is to supplement the intake of vitamins and /or minerals from the normal diet.

Food is defined as "any substance, whether processed, semi-processed or raw, which is intended for human consumption, and includes drink, chewing gum, and any substance which have been used in the manufacture, preparation or treatment of food but does not include cosmetics or tobacco or substances used only as drugs." Codex Proposed Draft Guidelines for Vitamins and Mineral Food Supplements guidelines apply in those jurisdictions where vitamin and mineral food supplement products are regulated as foods. The classification of these vitamin and mineral supplements is left to national regulations. Relevant groups are the Codex Committee on Nutrition and Foods for Special Dietary Uses, the Codex Alimentarius Commission, and the Joint FAO/WHO Food Standards Programme.

EU

All food containing voluntarily added vitamins and minerals to replace nutritive value lost during processing, to produce substitute foods and to fortify foods are covered by the Vitamins and Minerals in Foods Proposal 2003/0262 COD; It is proposed that the Standing Committee on Food Chain and Animal Health regulate the level of vitamins and minerals allowed in food. Fortified foods are included in a register. Regulation on labelling, advertising and presentation will be put in place.

Germany

Foods supplemented with vitamins, amino acids, minerals and other nutritive substances are classified as fortified foods in Germany. Inclusion of vitamins in food is regulated by the *Food Act* (LMG 1974). This *Food Act* allows vitamin A and D in food. The other regulation is the *Vitamin-Verordnung 1942*, describing vitamin C, vitamin B_1, vitamin B_6, vitamin B_{12}, phanthetonate, vitamin E and niacin and some minerals in food. Jurisprudence cites that vitamins can be added up to three times the RDA (Recommended Daily Allowance), without regulation. Discussions on amounts of supplements to be allowed will follow the proposed EU regulation 2003/0262. Bundes Ministerium fur Verbraucherschutz, Erharung und Landwirtschaft (Federal Ministry for Consumer Protection, Nutrition and Agriculture) is administering the German Regulations. All fortified foods are registered with the Ministry of Foods, and listed in the "Food Book."

USA

In the USA, fortified foods include the addition of vitamins or minerals and others. The FDA regulates this addition through food standards and food additive regulations. These Regulations control what nutrients can be added to food. Substitute foods must be nutritionally equivalent to food replaced or food must be labelled Aimitation." The Center for Food Safety and Applied Nutrition, Office of Food Additive Safety, USA Food and Drug Administration, US Department of Health and Human Services is the regulatory body responsible for the regulation of fortified foods. Assessment is needed by this body to obtain pre-market approval for food additives.

4.4   Strategy Approach for Prioritized Policy Research Needs

Prioritized policy needs in regulating of natural health products depend on two major factors. One factor is the extent to which the *Natural Health Products Regulations* are solidly in place and have matured in terms of smoothing out any hindrances to their working efficiently from the viewpoint of all stakeholders. For instance, the NHPD should have experience in product licencing for each of the levels of evidence for NHPs. The administration of these regulations should be effective and efficient before major trade initiatives such as international agreements are initiated. The discussion is focused on both trade and safety issues.

4.4.1   Trade Considerations

NHPs comprise a large business sector both in Canada and elsewhere in the world. Consumers are buying these products in record volumes all in an effort to make themselves feel better, to get better, and to possibly live longer. The NHP industry shows no signs of fading. Currently poised above the billion-dollar mark in Canada alone, surveys reveal that more than 50% of Canadians are consuming NHPs. Estimates in the United States compiled by the Natural Foods Merchandiser put the sales of natural products and supplements in 2003 at more than $20.5 billion.

The overall aim for trade development should be to look for methods and means for further harmonization with trading partners and to develop MRAs. The main policy research area for trade lies in the development of processes and approaches to produce an MRA or similar agreements. Currently Canada has not developed MRAs in the NHP sector. Therefore, cost-benefit analyses should be conducted to be able to assess which aspects of international harmonization initiatives should be pursued and at an optimal rate. It will be necessary to have a managed strategy with respect to international harmonization. One approach is to select specific pilot projects in priority areas and assess these as they develop and meet identified time-frames. In this way, a baseline assessment of the costs and benefits of harmonization in the international arena can be calculated.

In May 2003 the EACSR was established by the Canadian federal government to provide an external perspective and expert advice on how the federal government needs to redesign its regulatory approach for Canada in the twenty-first century. The EACSR is pursuing three inter-related activity streams:

- Regulatory strategy for the twenty-first century;
- Priority sectors and areas for reform; and
- Current regulatory issues.

The EACSR vision is for governments, citizens and businesses to work together to build a national regulatory system that enables Canadians to take advantage of new knowledge and supports Canada's participation in an international economy. The three components of the vision are trust, innovation and protection. The EACSR can contribute to an improved regulatory strategy for the future by providing strategic advice on clear objectives and principles to maximize the contribution of regulations to Canada's social, environmental and economic objectives. For instance, in the area of international regulatory cooperation the EACSR will examine the following areas of inquiry:

- Under what circumstances can Canada best pursue its national interests by engaging in bilateral or multinational regulatory cooperation?
- Under what circumstances and criteria should Canada rely on the regulatory threshold or standards developed by other countries or international organizations?
- How can Canada improve its regulatory relationship with the United States and what impact will alignment with the United States have on Canadian flexibility to work with other trading partners?

Therefore the work of the EACSR will be important in the development of any Canadian international trade initiatives and safety strategies for NHPs. One important area of development is performance measurement and the need to produce a more rigorous process for setting and reporting on regulatory performance.

An important international trade agreement for Canada is the North American Free Trade Agreement. This is a trade agreement between Canada, the United States and Mexico that encourage free trade between these North American countries. Implemented on January 1, 1994, this agreement is based on the concept that removing as many tariffs as possible between these North American countries will increase trade within this region benefitting each other's economies.

Another important international trade agreement was the General Agreement on Tariffs and Trade (GATT). This agreement was signed in 1947 and its purpose is to promote global trade between members through a reduction in tariffs. The creation of GATT and its amendments up to 1994 laid the framework for the formation of the World Trade Organization in 1995.

Regulatory cooperation between countries and blocs of countries means going beyond the simple exchange of information and personnel. It is now going in the direction of sharing issues, the development and implementation of globally cooperative solutions and the establishment of Mutual Recognition Agreements and Memoranda of Understanding (MOU).

4.4.2 TRADE STRATEGIES

In developing trade strategies, the NHPD cannot work alone. Trade issues include many sensitivities that go beyond the NHPD area of influence. First and foremost, the Department of Foreign Affairs and International Trade (DFAIT) should be consulted by the NHPD because the DFAIT is normally the lead department in dealing with international issues.

Discussions with DFAIT would focus on first researching and then developing a series of strategies for natural health product trade that could include:

- the development of MRAs;
- the use of vehicles such as the NAFTA to initiate pilot projects and eventually enter into agreements;
- bilateral discussions with selected countries (e.g., China, the United States);
- consideration of the most effective approach to working with the United States as it is Canada's largest trading partner. For example, the consideration of expanding the discussions and exploratory programs through such vehicles as the North American Tripartite discussions under the Food and Drugs

area is a possible initiative;
- creation of an International Harmonization Committee specifically for herbals with the World Health Organization or the European Agency for the Evaluation of Medicinal Products (EMEA), Ad Hoc Working Group on Herbal Medicinal Products and then form a subcommittee and choose compatible Canadian partners (e.g., Australia, France, United States) with which to work on pilot projects.

In the research and development of the trade strategies, the following elements may affect an overall Canadian strategy for NHP trade:

a) From a Canadian perspective, the *NHP Regulations* may ensure a demand for Canadian approved products entering the large American market. American regulatory standards are less rigorous and many American products would therefore not be able to enter Canada. Differences in regulatory requirements could become an important trade issue. One approach could include monitoring the Canadian NHP trade for a select number of products into the United States and then observing how quickly their dietary supplements regulations are strengthened and approaches Canada's. Canada's NHP Regulations could serve as a best practice to assist and advise the United States as they change their regulations to facilitate Canadian NHP products into the United States.

b) From the point of view of volume of products exchanged or similarity of regulatory systems, Canada has three main NHP trading partners: the United States, the EU and Australia. One possible approach to working with the EU, one consideration is for Canada to choose a EU member (e.g., the United Kingdom) with the view of eventually attaining an MRA. Thus, if Canada succeeds in obtaining an MRA with the United Kingdom, it will have an entrance to other EU countries such as France and Germany through the United Kingdom under EU Directives that allow entry through one Member State.

c) Another approach is for Canada to work with the regulatory tripartite group of the United States, Mexico and Canada under NAFTA to begin the MRA process from that point. As a second step, the tripartite group could engage the EU in initial pilot MRA proceedings. This approach gives Canada the weight of NAFTA in dealing with the large EU.

d) Another flow of trade goods could be from the United States to Canada and then to the EU; this would depend on which of the above scenarios is initially chosen.

e) Overall the priority should be to establish MRAs and trade with those countries that have the best standards (e.g., Australia). It is important to work with those countries that do not have rigorous standards but who export NHPs that are in demand in Canada (e.g., China, Hong Kong) in a careful, step wise, and confidence building manner (especially in the areas of compliance and enforcement).

f) The Management Advisory Committee has advised gathering further NHP regulatory information concerning Japan, Italy, Brazil, Mexico and other South American countries. This would allow a wider range of countries as possible future candidates for MRAs.

4.4.3 SAFETY STRATEGIES

Strategies and policy research areas which incorporate the product safety aspects of NHPs would ideally include the elements of the NHPD regulatory framework which ensure safe NHPs for Canadians (e.g., Product Licencing, Standards of Evidence, Good Manufacturing Practices, Site Licencing and Adverse Reaction Reporting) as well as other topics such as Good Agricultural Practices. One common strategy for all these safety assessment areas is for the NHPD to acquire all the latest information and policies from national and international organizations on new initiatives and changes to existing guidelines, standards and organizational changes. The NHPD should be participating on relevant committees and working groups at the international level to gain first hand information as well as actively contributing to areas of regulatory interest. One example is the Organization for Economic Cooperation and Development (OECD) committee on the Guidelines for Testing of Chemicals.

Policy priorities will be constantly changing in this NHP regulatory area and it would be useful to have a group in the NHPD that is commissioned to gather policy intelligence and coordinate the gathering of this intelligence while at the same time feeding the key pieces of information back into the NHPD for the use of all staff. For instance, any international changes in the Standards of Evidence that NHPD uses will be important information for the NHPD product evaluators. Canada should not only look at the regulations, guidelines and policies of the current major trading partners in NHPs, but also keep abreast of changes in the regulations, guidelines and policies as well as evaluate the direction of change in countries such as Japan, Taiwan, Mexico and the South American countries, as the supplies and markets for NHPs in Canada will likely shift with changing conditions and consumer demands.

In the area of Product Licencing, policy research should include the continued monitoring of Canada's main trading partners as well as emerging trade partners and partners with unique or novel Product Licencing systems. The Canadian NHP Standards of Evidence should be harmonized as much as possible with internationally recognized organizations such as the United States Agency for Healthcare Research and Quality and the OECD Guidelines for the Testing of Chemicals.

In the area of Standards of Evidence, the NHPD has chosen an evidence evaluation framework that is based on categories developed by the United States Agency for Healthcare Research and Quality. It is considered that this is the correct strategy. This framework was adopted with minor modifications by the Australian Therapeutic Goods Administration, the European Agency for the Evaluation of Medicinal Products and the World Health Organization. Both the areas of types of evidence and types of claims are important research areas for policy work. By having the NHPD participate on the appropriate working groups and committees, the NHPD will not only stay informed but will have the opportunity to positively influence future directions in this area.

Participation in the OECD committee on the Guidelines for Testing of Chemicals as well as relevant committees on Good Laboratory Practices is an important area of policy research. The NHPD must be fully aware of new directions in animal testing and should participate in these committees or, at the very least, be fully current with new developments.

Good Manufacturing Practices (GMP) and Site Licencing provides other areas of possible policy research. Those countries that possess GMP compliance programs, once identified, must be examined for the details of their standards, regulatory directives, inspection resources, inspection procedures, inspection standards, enforcement powers and procedures, alert and crisis systems, analytical capability, surveillance programs and quality management systems. In addition, the NHPD should examine the possibility of developing ongoing communications between the NHPD and other national regulatory authorities that meet Canada's regulatory standards for safety and quality. Possible confidence building mechanisms should be examined.

Good Agricultural Practices is an important area for policy research that has not been explored to any great extent by Canada. The GAP policies of international groups and Canada's main trading partners should be analyzed. Several trading partners also require that plant and animal material be produced under GAP. Such GAPs ensure that production takes place under "standardized" conditions to allow for optimum product quality and product safety. European countries, Canada and the United States do not require the primary production of NHPs to be covered by a GAP.

In many countries, a close equivalent to GAP is the voluntary Organic Certification, which is sanctioned through nationally and internationally recognized standards (ISO 65 with National standards, USDA - NOP programs with standards, and European standards and regulations according to EEC 2092/91). As Canada does not require plant production according to a GAP standard for NHPs or any agricultural or horticultural commodity, the country's food safety and environmental enforcement are based on many different programs of the Canadian Food Inspection Agency and other (Provincial) Authorities. Canada may wish to investigate a nationwide program for agricultural production of NHPs, and to compare the framework of Canadian agricultural, horticultural and food safety regulations with the GAP requirements in other Canadian major trading partners.

Adverse Reaction Reporting is another very important policy research area. On June 23, 2004, the World Health Organization (WHO) announced new WHO Guidelines to promote the proper use of alternative medicines. The NHPD participated in the development of this document. These guidelines report that, in a survey of many of the world's countries, adverse drug reactions to alternative medicines have more than doubled in three years. The Adverse Reaction Reporting area is one that must be continually developed and supported. Continued policy research in this area that builds on the relevant components in this latest WHO document is necessary to develop the post market surveillance of Canadian NHPs. Relating the main areas and recommendations of this WHO document to the House of Commons Standing Committee on Health fifty-three recommendations, produced in 1999, would indicate further policy research areas to be supported. This includes the development of consumer information for the proper use of NHPs. Interactions of NHPs with pharmaceuticals should also be a priority area for policy research. The current status of NHPs in this area should be known and shared internationally.

Perception of health risks is an important area of policy research that can affect the overall scope for international collaboration. For instance, in areas where the perceived health risks are low, harmonization of Product Licencing, Standards of Evidence, Site Licencing or Good Manufacturing Practices may be easier to achieve than for products that have a high level of perceived health risk. In situations where the perceived health risks for an NHP is high, Canadians may favour decision-making in Canada.

The NHPD should consider adopting useful systems pertinent to NHP regulation that have been developed by the United States Food and Drug Administration and the European Agency for the Evaluation of Medicinal Products, since consistency with policies in other jurisdictions would be desirable in a global environment. The NHPD should strive to align, as much as possible, its rules with the widely accepted International Conference on Harmonization recommendations for those NHPs that fall in this area.

4.4.4 MUTUAL RECOGNITION AGREEMENTS

It is an important for Canada to develop a system of MRAs in the NHP sector. Mutual Recognition Agreements can be used strategically to optimize trade for Canada while assuring the safety, efficacy and effectiveness of natural health products purchased in Canada and assisting in reducing the regulatory burden for industry.

Mutual Recognition Agreements are vehicles that are used within the context of international trade. These are specific trade agreements designed to facilitate trade by eliminating or reducing trade barriers between two countries. An MRA is a bilateral agreement to accept testing, evaluation or inspection decisions of a regulatory authority in the exporter's jurisdiction, as long as they are equivalent to those which would have been made in the importing jurisdiction. An MRA establishes a solid framework for regulatory cooperation between regulators of products. An MRA does not require the harmonization of regulatory requirements, but focuses instead on the capabilities and the equivalency of processes and procedures for each country to reach the same evaluation, testing or inspection decision. Mutual recognition must be carefully defined by the affected Parties. Complete mutual recognition of another nation's regulatory decisions means that we would give up our sovereign right to make our own decisions. This type of mutual recognition is one that would not likely be used. However, Canada could accept mutual recognition of test data developed according to well defined scientific protocols. This may work out well for those natural health products associated with low health risks.

Mutual Recognition Agreements can foster the development of a more effective international system of natural health product development and trade by using the resources available to both Parties' regulatory authorities in the most effective manner. For instance, the NHPD can insist that a "bidirectional" alert system be an integral part of an MRA for the area of Adverse Reaction Reports. This would then ensure a timely and efficient process to protect the health and safety of Canadians.

Following are important principles that would be useful to the NHPD in the development of MRAs for NHPs:

- the health and safety of the populations of each country would be paramount in any agreement;
- MRAs are to form part of the framework in which regulatory decisions are made within each decision and MRAs do not override the existing regulatory regimes;
- participation by a regulatory authority (such as NHPD) in the MRA will not require that authority to relinquish its jurisdictional authority;
- the successful completion of a confidence building exercise and a positive evaluation of its results is a necessary first step;
- for natural health products, regulatory authorities with adverse reaction reporting, product licencing, marketing authorization and manufacturing authorization programs would be first considered;
- there must be an agreed system to ensure a current and timely flow of information on all regulatory changes by both Parties; in addition, both Parties would consult before adopting these changes to ensure a continuing equivalence of regulatory actions;
- all terms in the agreement including items such as product licencing and marketing authorization would be defined.

Mutual Recognition Agreements should aim at a better utilization of resources and reducing any duplication of regulatory effort. Generally, Canada should be proactive in the development of MRAs when there is a competitive advantage to gain or where we could share the costs associated with the approval processes such as product licencing.

Canada should also be selective in choosing trading partners for an MRA. For instance, the United States is a natural geographical partner but their regulatory processes do not cover the essential area of product licencing for natural health products. Another factor affecting the development of trade with the United States is that it has a very unstable regulatory environment because Congress frequently enacts legislation in response to special interest groups. Australia would appear to be an excellent partner for forming an MRA with Canada as their regulatory system for natural health products is similar to Canada's. Further, their system is more developed than Canada's and the NHPD can learn from Australia's experience and developmental lessons. If the safety requirements present in the Australian NHP regulatory framework are at par with or surpass the safety requirements of the Canadian regulatory framework, then any initial mutual recognition processes would sensibly include Australia in initial pilot projects.

Working at the direct level of the regulatory scientist is one way to share the burden of product evaluation. This can be used in natural health products of higher risk. Scientists can pool information and resources and share conclusions but can make the final approval specific to their own country. This approach spreads the workload and preserves the sovereign right to decide whether to accept or reject a product submission. This is a work reduction process that can be implemented rapidly. For instance, if there are a small number of Australian high risk natural health products that have also been submitted to the NHPD, this may serve as the basis for a common review by both Canada and Australia. The confidentiality of proprietary information may be a constraint in this case unless the industry applicant approves the joint process or unless an administrative agreement makes the Australian evaluator an employee of the NHPD.

The formal government-to-government arrangements would primarily occur in relation to harmonization and mutual recognition of testing protocols and scientific data. These are usually developed very slowly and in stages of confidence building. Agreements are most easily made in areas involving quantitative testing as opposed to areas involving subjective assessments. Agreements on standard methods of testing often pave the way for harmonization and mutual recognition and these protocols are most easily applied for quantitative testing. This approach is based on the principle that scientists can be relied on to report their test data accurately and honestly, especially when standard protocols allow others to carefully check their findings. Thus the international sharing of data is greatly facilitated if procedures are standardized.

A further approach is the sharing of a reviewer's summary of the data. To share such documents, a high level of trust and mutual respect must exist between the countries. At the very least, the sharing of summary data can serve as an aid to the reviewers who assess the product safety of NHPs. Finally, when full mutual recognition has been achieved over a long period of time, there can be sharing of the detailed conclusions for a reviewed product. Normally this approach is used for low risk products.

Post evaluation surveillance is an excellent method of international work sharing as most regulatory agencies are generally willing to share information on safety and efficacy once the products have been approved. Acceptance of common electronic formats for product submissions is a further area of possible agreement between countries. For this area Canada should harmonize with existing international formats. Active communications to the industry and general public concerning the specific regulatory program and the use of international collaboration would be mandatory. Using foreign approvals or rejections are other sources of information that would assist the NHPD in accomplishing its work. The NHPD should contribute to and access international databases such as that of post market surveillance as much as possible.

CHAPTER 5

CONCLUSIONS, IMPLICATIONS, AND RECOMMENDATIONS

5.1 LEGISLATIVE AND LITERATURE REVIEW

This Legislative and Literature review reveals a fast-paced change and revision of national and international regulations for NHPs such as herbals, vitamins, minerals and homeopathic medicines. Many changes in the European countries were precipitated by the implementation of European Union Directives.

5.2 CONSULTATION PROCESS WITH NHPD, MANAGEMENT ADVISORY COMMITTEE

Several MAC members commented that the Comparison document which they had reviewed was well done. MAC suggestions that covered areas outside the terms of reference of the Comparison document included; broadening the comparison analysis to other countries, considering a wider range of self-care health products, performing an analysis on the trends in manufacturing, increase of sales and possible expansion of product base for companies whose countries had revised regulations and, for the USA, analysing the regulatory situation for NHPs versus the over-the-counter self-care health products as industry would want to be assured of a level playing field. Overall, the MAC suggestions were very useful in the development of the strategy document.

5.3   COMPARISON OF REGULATORY FRAMEWORKS

From this literature and legislative review it can be concluded that Canada's main trading partners have varied regulatory systems, ranging from strict EU-Germany model to the less rigorous USA model. The comparison with Canada's regulations indicates that Canada's regulations are rigorous but not quite as rigorous as the EU-Germany regulations. Canada's Asian trading partners have written strict regulations in many cases, but the enforcement of the regulations is sometimes questionable and therefore depending on the enforcement of their regulations, the safety, quality and efficacy of their NHPs may be in question. This will affect the quality of the products imported into Canada. With the Canadian NHP Regulations, a company can obtain an NHP product licence in one of two ways: by attestation to a monograph in Health Canada's Compendium and by a full scientific assessment for which data to support the product's safety, quality and health claims are submitted. It is interesting to note that by harmonizing the Canadian NHP Standards of Evidence (SOE) framework with the SOE framework of other countries, international trade in NHP's could be facilitated.

On the whole, the definitions of NHPs deal with their functionality, where the substance in certain cases modifies the conditions required under the functionality. For several trading partners, all NHPs fall under the concept of "drug" or "medicine". This is the case for the European Union and therefore generally covers Germany, France and the United Kingdom. China and India use the functionality principle and classify NHPs as drugs or food. However, China also recognizes Traditional Chinese Medicine and health food products as separate classes. The United States and Australia base their definitions on substances and their workings and not as much on functionality principles.

The review of the regulations in Canada's main trading partners reveals that Canada's licensing and registration is comparable with the licencing requirements of the EU and EU member states. India requires registration and licensing of all NHPs and China and Hong Kong requires registration and licensing of products classified in the drugs category. Australia requires registration of some NHPs and listing of others, while the USA does not require registration or licencing for "current" dietary supplements. For other NHP products such as homeopathic medicines the USA does require registration.

All of Canada's main trading partners require standards of evidence to ensure that any substance is considered safe for use as a self-care product. In most countries this is the same standard of evidence used for drugs or medicinal products. Although the USA considers some NHPs as dietary supplements, they do not require standards of evidence. Most of Canada's main trading partners in NHPs require site licensing as the products are considered as drugs or medicine. The EU and its member states require site licensing procedures for all products, as does Australia, Hong Kong and India. Some of Canada's trading partners do not require site licensing for vitamins and minerals as long as they are not classified as drugs or medicines.

All of Canada's trading partners require that manufacturers of drugs or medicines follow GMP practices. For dietary supplements (DS), the USA currently requires GMPs applicable to food products. However, the USA has recently proposed GMPs specific to DS and for the other NHPs, the drug GMPs apply. Several countries, not including Canada, have implemented Good Agricultural Practices. The GAP may be used as a trade barrier by Canadian trading partners. It is recommended that Canada's position on GAP be reviewed.

The adverse reaction reporting for NHPs in Canada's main trading partners varies from full reporting for all drugs, homeopathic medicine, and vitamins and minerals, (e.g., European Countries and EC Directive; China), to voluntary reporting requirements (e.g., Australia, USA) and no requirements (e.g., India).

Of Canada's trading partners, only the USA and Germany have established regulations for fortified foods. Germany establishes which additives (vitamins and minerals) can be included and how much. The USA requires a pre-market approval of food additives, and Australia only allows vitamins and minerals in foods that conform to their standards. Several international bodies including the EC and the Codex Alimentarius are drafting regulations regarding the inclusion of vitamins and minerals (and other substances) in foods.

5.4 STRATEGY APPROACH FOR PRIORITIZED POLICY RESEARCH NEEDS

The priority policy research areas fall in two main categories: the safety of the products being manufactured and sold to Canadians and ways to facilitate trade between countries.

The main strategy approach for trade lies in the development of processes and approaches to produce MRAs or similar agreements. The use of vehicles such as the NAFTA to initiate pilot projects and eventually enter into agreements is another strategy. The fact that the United States is Canada's largest trading partner should be foremost in formulating any Canadian NHP trade strategy. The strategic use of bilateral discussions with selected countries (e.g., China, the United States) is suggested. A further strategy is to create an International Harmonization Committee specifically for herbals with the World Health Organization or the European Agency for the Evaluation of Medicinal Products, Ad Hoc Working Group on Herbal Medicinal Products.

Policy research areas which incorporate the aspects of health and safety evaluation of the products submitted for approval by the NHPD would ideally encompass the elements of the NHPD regulatory framework (e.g., Product Licencing, Standards of Evidence, Good Manufacturing Practices, Site Licencing and Adverse Reaction Reporting). The strategies for this area include ensuring that the NHPD is in a position to deal internationally by having a reasonable amount of experience in selected areas such as Standards of Evidence. This would mean that the NHPD would have completed product submissions for all the levels of evidence.

Good Agricultural Practices comprise an area for which very little policy work has been accomplished and this is suggested as an area to develop. Adverse Reaction Reporting is an important policy research area that should be further developed. Another important policy area is the interaction between NHPs and pharmaceuticals.

A further strategy would be to ensure that cost-benefit analyses should be conducted to assess which aspects of international harmonization initiatives should be pursued and at what rate. It will be necessary to have a managed strategy with respect to international harmonization.

The listed areas of investigation, research and trade development are prioritized based on their effectiveness and ease of implementation. By following the prioritized list, NHPD's experience and expertise will accumulate and the more difficult strategies will benefit from this experience. It is concluded that the following priorities should be considered:

- NHPD obtains experience with the implementation and administration of the current regulations and fine-tunes the process;
- NHPD reviews the work of the EACSR as this will be important in the development of any Canadian international trade initiatives and safety strategies for NHPs. One important area of development is performance measurement and the need to produce a more rigorous process for setting and reporting on regulatory performance.

- NHPD investigates and keeps track of the regulatory and guideline changes for Canada's trading partners, including the countries reviewed for this work, and those that potentially could become major trading partners such as Japan, Taiwan, Mexico and the South American countries. This is based on the major effect that small changes in regulations can have on the overall flow of NHPs in and out of Canada;
- NHPD researches product safety-related regulations such as those administered by the Canadian Food Inspection Agency and compares those with gaps in the implementation of safety related regulations of several of Canada's trading partners;
- NHPD investigates the level of regulatory enforcement in countries such as China, Hong Kong and Taiwan to ensure safe and effective products entering Canada;
- NHPD contacts DFAIT and develops a framework for assistance in international trade in NHPs;
- NHPD selects a country with a regulatory system similar to Canada's (e.g., Australia) and uses this collaboration to develop MRAs on a pilot scale basis;
- NHPD reviews the relationship with the EU and with the United States in relation to trade volume including import and export, potential for trade restrictions based on differences of regulations, and ease of access to Canada's foreign markets;
- NHPD researches and develops a pilot project to develop protocols for accepting American produced NHPs into Canada, and Canadian authorized products into the United States, using the MRA model, both within the NAFTA and outside the NAFTA framework; and
- NHPD researches and develops a mutual relationship allowing import and export of NHPs to and from the EU through one of the EU's Member States (e.g., the United Kingdom), using the MRA model.

Whether for trade or safety, considerable experience exists in Health Canada for the development and ongoing consideration of strategic policy research in creating MRAs and harmonization initiatives for various health products. Therefore, this expertise and experience should be used to facilitate the work of the NHPD.

Reference List:
International Natural Health Products
Regulatory Literature Review

Artiges, A.(1991). What are the legal requirements for the use of phytopharmaceutical drugs in France? *Journal of Ethnopharmacology*, 32 (1-3), April; 231-234.

Baker, S.(2002). Regulatory concerns within the UK. *International Journal of Aromatherapy*, 12: 1, 60-61.

Bast, A., Chandler, R.F., Choy, P.C., Delmulle, L.M., Gruenwald, J., Halkes, S.B.A., Keller, K., Koeman, J.H., Peters,P., Przyrembel, H., de Ree, E.M., Renwick, A.G. & Vermeer, I.T.M. (2002). Botanical health products, positioning and requirements for effective and safe use. *Environmental Toxicology and Pharmacology*, 12: 4, 195-211.

Biffignandi, P.M. & Carletto, L. (2000). The new attitude of the European regulatory authorities about herbal medicinal products. *Drug Information Journal*, 34: 3, 801-808.

Blumenthal, M. (2004). Congress Increasingly Active on Herbs and Dietary Supplements: Durbin's Bill Intends to Clamp Down on Supplementary Safety while Hatch and Harkin Propose More Funding for FDA Enforcement of DSHEA. HerbalGram, 61: 56-59.

Boon, H.(2003). Regulation of Natural Health Products in Canada. *Clinical Research and Regulatory Affairs*, 20(3):299-312.

Briggs, C. & Norrie, O.(2003). Regulation of Herbal and Homeopathic Medicines, An Overview. *Pharm. Dev. Regul.*, (4):245-259.

Dvorkin, L. (2003). Regulation of Dietary Supplements in the United States of America. *Clinical Research and Regulatory Affairs*, 20(3):313-325.

European Association of Proprietary Medicine Manufacturers (AES-

GP) (1998). Herbal medicinal products in the European Union. *European Commission.*

European Council for Classical Homeopathy (1999). Homeopathy in Ten Countries: Survey of ten countries where homeopathy is being practised. Available at : *http://www.homeopathy-ecch.org/survey. html* and accessed Feb. 10, 2004.

Gaedcke, F. & Steinhoff, B.(2003). Herbal Medicinal Products. Scientific and Regulatory Basis for Development, Quality Assurance and Marketing Authorisation. Medpharm Scientific Publishers, Balogh International, Inc.

Keller, K. (2002). Herbal medicinal products in the European Union. *WHO Drug Information,* 16: 2, 115-118.

Keller, K. (1996). Herbal medicinal products in Germany and Europe: experiences with national and European assessment. *Drug Information Journal,* 30:4, 933-948.

Keller, K.(1991). Legal requirements for the use of phytopharmaceutical drugs in the Federal Republic of Germany. *J. Ethnopharmacology,* April; 32(1-2): 225-229.

Mukherjee, P.K.(2003). Exploring Botanicals in Indian System of Medicine-Regulatory Perspectives. *Clinical Research and Regulatory Affairs,* 20(3):249-264.

Pan, D.(1997). Regulation of The People's Republic of China: A Comprehensive Analysis of PRC Food and Drug Regulatory Structures and Laws. Harvard University , Food and Drug Law.Available at *http://leda.law.harvard.edu/leda/data/168/dpan.pdf* and accessed on Feb. 14, 2004.

Ray, S.(1998). Botanical Products Regulation: Remedying the Unstable Dietary Supplement-Drug Divide. Third Year Paper, Harvard Law School. Available at: *http://leda.law.harvard.edu/leda/data/231/ sray.pdf* and accessed on Feb. 10, 2004.

Scholten, W.K. and Halkes, S.B.A. (2001). Introducing a system for the assessment of quality, safety, and efficacy of herbal medicinal products in the Netherlands. *Drug Information Journal,* 35:2, 461-468.

Steinhoff, B. (2003). Regulatory Status of Herbal Medicinal Products in Germany. *Clinical Research and Regulatory Affairs,* 20(3):265-284.

Steinhoff, B. (2002). The future of herbal medicinal products in Europe. *Zeitschrift fur Phytotherapie,* 23: 6, 282-285.

Steinhoff, B. (2002). E/S/C/O/P: Regulatory assessment of herbal medicinal products on a European level: the Herbal Medicinal Products Working Party. *Phytomedicine*, Oct; 9(7): 673.

Taller, J.B. (2003). Canada Issues Final Natural Health Product Regulations. *Herbalgram*, 60 :62-65.

West, S., King, V., Carey, T.S., Lohr, K.N., McKoy, N., Sutton, S.F., and Lux, L.(2002). Systems to rate the strength of scientific evidence. *Evidence Report/ Technology Assessment Number 47, AHRQ Publication No. 02-E016.* Rockville, MD: Agency for Healthcare Research and Quality.

Wiebe, A., Elford, N., Rogers, R., Dielman, S., Gausvik, A. and Wilsey,F. (2003). Herbal-Drug Interactions. *Mediscript Communications, Inc.*, 109 pps.

Wong, E. (2001). Regulation of Health Food in Overseas Places: Overall Comparison. Research and Library Services Division, Legislative Council Secretariat, Hong Kong. Available at *http://www.lego.gov.hk/english/index.htm* and accessed Feb. 16, 2004.

World Health Organization (2002). Proceedings of the Tenth International Conference of Drug Regulatory Authorities; Hong Kong, June 24-27. Available at: *http://www.who.int/medicines/library/qsm/icdra02_contents.shtml* and accessed on Feb.10, 2004.

World Health Organization (1998). Regulatory Situation of Herbal Medicines : A worldwide Review. Available at: *http://www.who.int/medicines/library/trm/who-trm-98-1/who-trm-98-1.pdf* and accessed Jan.20, 2004.

Wu, J. (2001). Regulation of Health Food in Hong Kong. Research and Library Services Division, Legislative Council Secretariat, Hong Kong. Available at *http://www.lego.gov.hk/english/index.htm* and accessed Feb. 16, 2004.

Table 1: Australia (Overview)

Products	Definition	Legislation/ Regulations/ Guidelines	Regulatory Agency	Marketing Authorization
Complementary medicines; a general term to describe a variety of health products.	A complementary medicine (CM) is defined as a therapeutic good consisting wholly or principally of one or more designated active ingredients, each of which has a clearly established identity and a traditional use; these include herbal medicines, homeopathic medicines, vitamins and mineral supplements, traditional medicines such as Ayurvedic medicines, traditional Chinese medicines, other nutritional supplements, and aromatherapy oils. Traditional use means use of the well documented & designated active ingredient according to the accumulated experience of traditional healthcare practitioners.	The Therapeutic Goods Act (TGA) 1989 (Section 52F, Definitions; Commonwealth of Australia. Therapeutic Goods Regulations 1990 as amended) and the Therapeutic Goods Regulations. This Act sets out the legal requirements for the import, manufacture and supply of medicines. These instruments define a complementary medicine and designate the types of active ingredients that may be used in these medicines. The TGA maintains the Australian Register of Therapeutic Goods (ARTG). CMs may be included on the ARTG as Listed (lower risk) or Registered Medicines; Registered medicines may be nonprescription (OTC) or available by prescription from an MD or authorized prescriber. A wide set of guidance documents exist for the overview of the regulations & regulatory components such as levels and kinds of evidence to support indications & claims, Good Manufacturing Practice & Pharmacovigilance.	Office of Complementary Medicines (created April 1999). Therapeutic Goods Administration (TGA), within the Australian Department of Human Services and Health. Uses expert committees such as the Traditional Medicines Evaluation Committee. The Complementary Medicines Evaluation Committee provides scientific and policy advice. Announced in Dec. 2003 was the future establishment of an Australian / New Zealand Agency to cover the regulation of drugs, medical devices and complementary medicines and is expected to begin in 2005.	Yes, from TGA: pre-market assessment of products and approval process covers safety, efficacy, claims, and product specifications. Reforms on pre-market assessment introduced in 1999. Further overall reforms of the Therapeutic Goods Act of 1989 adopted on May 27, 2003.
Fortified Foods	Regulations address vitamins and minerals. These are not permitted to be added to food unless permitted in regulations.	Australian New Zealand Food Standards Code (Volume 2). Standard 1.3.2: Vitamins and Minerals regulates the addition of vitamins & minerals to food.	Food Standards Australia New Zealand (FSANZ)	Regulatory Assessments required.

Table 2: Australia (Regulatory Components)

Products	Product Licensing/ Registration	Risk/Scientific Assessment/ Standards of Evidence (SOEs)	Site Licensing	Good Manufacturing Practices (GMPs)	Adverse Reaction Reporting
A complementary medicine (CM) is defined as a therapeutic good; these include herbal medicines, homeopathic medicines, vitamins and mineral supplements, traditional medicines, traditional Chinese medicines, other nutritional supplements, and aromatherapy oils.	Yes: The TGA maintains the Australian Register of Therapeutic Goods (ARTG). CMs may be included on the ARTG as Listed (lower risk) or Registered Medicines. Listed Medicines (LM) carry the designation AUST L, plus a unique number. Registered Medicines (RM) carry the designation AUST R plus a unique number and may be nonprescription (OTC) or available by prescription from an MD or authorized prescriber. Registration is a more detailed process than listing and it requires pre-market evidence of safety and efficacy. Indications and claims for LMs are not subject to pre-market evaluation; e.g. Health Maintenance, Health Enhancement. Indications/claims for RMs relate to treatment, management, cure of disease/disorders.	Yes: LM evaluation uses a process that aims to ensure any substance approved for use is of low risk. Four types of data are used to support safety evaluation in LMs: Biological activity, Toxicology, Clinical Trials and Adverse reactions. RM evaluation uses standards of quality, safety and efficacy as required for OTC and prescription medicines. For identified risks or potential health risks or potential restrictions may be imposed such as label advisory information, dosage restrictions, route of administration or plant part and/ or restriction of the form in which the substance can be used.	Yes: Australian manufacturers of medicinal products for human use must hold a manufacturing license. It is an offence, carrying heavy penalties, to manufacture therapeutic goods without such a license, unless the goods are exempt from this requirement. License holders are required to comply with the manufacturing principles of the Act. These principles require compliance with Good Manufacturing Practice (GMP).	Yes: Australian manufacturers are required to comply with the Australian Code of GMP for Medicinal Products. The Code covers requirements in: Quality Management, Personnel, Premises and Equipment, Documentation, Production and Quality Control. Pre-licensing audits and, thereafter, regular on-site audits of manufacturers are conducted	Yes: Monitoring of adverse reactions to CMs is conducted using a Blue Card System that is a voluntary reporting system: Sponsors of all medicines in the ARTG are under an obligation to report adverse reactions to the TGA. These reports are entered into the Adverse Drug Reaction Reporting System database. Serious reaction reports are reviewed by TGA MD and are also reviewed by the Adverse Drug Reaction Advisory Committee. Summary Reports for CMs are also sent to the Complementary Medicines Evaluation Committee for advice.

Table 3: Canada (Overview)

Products	Definition	Legislation/Regulations/Guidelines	Regulatory Agency	Marketing Authorization
Natural Health Products (NHPs); a general term to describe a variety of health products.	Natural Health Products are defined in Schedule 1 of the NHP Regulations as: 1) a plant or a plant material, an alga, a bacterium, a fungus or a non-human animal matter; 2) an extract or isolate of a substance described in item 1, the primary molecular structure of which it had prior to its extraction or isolation; 3) any of the following vitamins: biotin, folate, niacin, pantothenic acid, riboflavin, thiamine, vitamin A, vitamin B_6, vitamin B_{12}, vitamin C, vitamin D, vitamin E; 4) an amino acid; 5) an essential fatty acid; 6) a synthetic duplicate described in any of terms 2 to 5; 7) a mineral; 8) a probiotic.	NHPs classified as a subset of drugs under the Food and Drugs Act but under separate new regulations. Natural Health Products Regulations. Food and Drugs Act. Regulations came into effect January 1, 2004. Will take six years to fully implement the Regulations. A set of guidance documents exist for the overview of the regulations & the components of the regulatory framework such as product licensing, site licensing & Adverse Reaction Reporting.	Natural Health Products Directorate (NHPD), Health Canada.	Yes, from NHPD; pre-market review and approval process covers safety, efficacy, claims, and product specifications.
Fortified Foods	Fortification is the addition of essential nutrients, especially vitamins and minerals, at levels above those normally found in the particular type of food to which they have been added, to address a deficiency or inadequate intake of the nutrient in the diet of people. Vitamins and minerals may also be added to restore those lost due to food processing, to make a substitute food nutritionally equivalent to the food for which it is substituting, or to make a special purpose food, including sole sources of nutrition.	Food and Drug Regulations, Part D, Division 3. Legislation for the addition of vitamins and minerals to ordinary foods is of the "General Permission" type. General Permission refers to the situation where nutrient addition is regulated by legislation which specifies the foods and/or nutrients permitted and also the levels of the nutrients which might be permitted. In Canada's case, the allowed nutrients and their levels are specified in foods.	Food Directorate, Health Products and Food Branch, Health Canada	N/A

Table 4: Canada (Regulatory Components)

Products	Product Licensing	Risk/Scientific Assessments/ Standards of Evidence (SOEs)	Site Licensing	Good Manufacturing Practices (GMPs)	Adverse Reaction Reporting
Natural Health Products (NHPs): defined in Schedule 1 of the NHP Regulations (see Canada Overview table) a general term to describe a variety of health products. Includes herbs, homeopathics, vitamins, minerals, nutritional supplements, probiotics and essential fatty acids.	Yes: Regulations require an individual (e.g. manufacturer, importer or distributor) to obtain a product license (PL) prior to selling an NHP in Canada. Sufficient information must be submitted to support the safety and efficacy of the product. Types of evidence submitted will determine the types of claims allowed. Claims can be: structure/ function, risk-reduction, or therapeutic claims associated with drugs. The product's medicinal and non-medicinal ingredients are to be submitted and also listed on the product label.	Yes: Standards of Evidence outline the types, strength, quality and quantity of evidence required to support NHP safety and efficacy. Based on ingredients and claims, NHPs can be divided into two categories: traditional (those that have been used for at least 50 years) and non-traditional. Five types of evidence may be submitted. These range from references to traditional uses to randomized control clinical trials. The type of evidence submitted is to be appropriate to the claims used. The totality of evidence is assessed for a particular product claim.	Yes: A manufacturer, packager, labeler or importer must obtain a site license (SL) which is evidence of GMP compliance. The Product License application must also include the SL numbers for all manufacturers, packagers, labelers or importers of the NHP. If the NHP is imported, the PL application must include similar information concerning all foreign sites performing any regulated activities.	Yes: GMPs measures are designed to ensure an effective overall approach to product quality control and risk management. They set appropriate standards and practices for product testing, manufacturing, storage, handling and distribution. The GMP Guidance Document outlines the requirements in detail for the manufacturing, packaging, labeling, importing and distributing of NHPs.	Yes: Regulations are set out for Reaction Reporting. A licensee has to produce a case report for each serious adverse reaction & serious unexpected adverse reaction to the NHP that occurs in Canada & produce summary reports on all adverse reactions to the NHPs that have occurred.

Table 5: People's Republic of China (Overview)

Products	Definition	Legislation/ Regulations/ Guidelines	Regulatory Agency	Marketing Authorization
Drugs	Articles that are used in the prevention, treatment and diagnosis of human diseases intended for the regulation of the physiological functions of human beings, for which indications, usage & dosage are established, including Chinese crude drugs, prepared slices of Chinese crude drugs, traditional Chinese medicine preparations, chemical drug substances & their preparations, antibiotics, biochemical drugs, radioactive pharmaceuticals, serum, vaccines, blood products & diagnostic agents.	Drug Administration Law of People's Republic of China (Promulgated by Order No. 45 of the President of the PRC on April 28, 2000 & effective as of Dec. 1, 2001) Regulations on the Enforcement of the Drug Administration Act, including: Provisional Measures for the Administration and Supervision of Drug Manufacturing, Certification Committee for Drug Registration, and the Administration of Drug Distribution, and Measures for the Administration of Drug Importation.	State Food and Drug Administration (SFDA), Ministry of Health (MOH), National Institute for the Control of Pharmaceutical and Biological Products; Statutory inspection institute and arbitration authority. National Pharmacopeia Committee, Centre for Drug Evaluation (for Drug registration), Certification Committee for Drugs (GLP (Good Laboratory Practice), GCP (Good Clinical Practice), GMP (Good Manufacturing Practices) & GAP (Good Agricultural Practices), Centre for Drug Reevaluation (drug catalogue).	Yes. With State Council Department responsible for health administration & the departments of the provinces, autonomous regions & municipalities under the direct control of the Central Government administering health (Article 25).
Traditional Chinese Medicine (TCM)	The Chinese legislation holds a special place for Traditional Chinese Medicines. TCM includes Chinese Medicinal Herbs (Dan Fang) and Chinese Prepared Medicines (Cheng Fang). These are recorded in the Pharmacopoeia of the People's Republic of China (PRC). There are over eighteen defined categories of Single Herbs and eighteen defined categories of Herbal Formulas in TCM.	Drug Administration Law of People's Republic of China : same as above. In addition there have been numerous regulations addressing TCM specifically, the most recent being the Regulations on Varieties Protection of TCM (State Council Regulation; Order No. 106; Effective Date 1993-01-01).	State Food and Drug Administration, Ministry of Health, Ministry of Commerce, China Chamber of Commerce of Medicines and Health Products Importers and Exporters and the State Administration of Traditional Chinese Medicines.	Yes as a broad interpretation of Article 25 of the Drug Administration Law of the PRC.
Food	Any product or raw material provided for people to eat or drink, as well as any product that has traditionally served as both food and medicament, with the exception of products used solely for medical purposes.	Food Hygiene Law of the People's Republic of China (Adopted at the 16 th Session of the Standing Committee of the Eighth National People's Congress on Oct. 30, 1995, promulgated by Decree No. 95 of the President, PRC on Oct. 30, 1995 and put into effect on the date of promulgation).	State Food and drug Administration (SFDA). Inspections are carried out by the qualified Food Hygiene Inspectors for the local Ministry of Health Administration Department.	Unclear.
Health Food Products	Any food product that has been tested and scientifically proven to have unmistakable and reliable health benefits and no acute, malignant, or chronic damaging effects to the human body. (The web site www.pregnatta.com has a news bulletin on health food supplements regulations in the PRC).	Same as above. Also, Administrative Provisions for Healthy Food. MOH regulation; Order No. 46; Promulgation Date; 1996-03-15; Effective Date; 1996-06-01. Guidelines provided for the application of health food status, the regulation of the production of health foods, and labeling, instructions pamphlets, advertising, and monitoring of health foods.	Ministry of Health	Yes.

Table 6: People's Republic of China (Regulatory Components)

Products	Product Licensing/Registration	Risk/Scientific Assessments/ Standards of Evidence (SOEs)	Site Licensing	Good Manufacturing Practices (GMPs)	Adverse Reaction Reporting
Health Food Products	Licensing is not mentioned, but the product must have claims verified and registered with MOH.	Yes	Unclear.	Ministry of Health Regulation: Order 46; Promulgation Date 1996-03-15; Effective: 1996-06-01; Guidelines for production, labeling, monitoring mentioned, GMPs not mentioned.	Yes.
Drugs	Yes, with the Centre for Drug Evaluation.	Yes	With GMP's in place it would appear that site licensing exists; not totally clear in regulations.	Drug Good Manufacturing Practice (GMP), Drug GMP Certification, Drug Good Laboratory Practice (GLP), Drug Good Clinical Practice (GCP), Green Trade Standard of Importing & Exporting Medicinal Plants & Preparations (Green Signs). Overseen by Certification Committee for Drugs.	Yes
Traditional Chinese Medicine (TCM)	Licensing is mentioned in short summaries of regulatory documents. There are provisions for two types of TCM Varieties Protection. Class 1 products have special efficacy in treating specific disease, are made from class 1 Wild Herbal Medicine Materials and can prevent &treat a specific disease. Class 2 products either match the Class 1 criteria, or have marked efficacy in treating specific disease & are made from the active ingredients or special formulations from natural herbal medicines.	Unclear.	Unclear.	Good Agricultural Practices (GAP) for Chinese Crude Drugs, Good Agricultural Practice for TCM Plants and Animals.	Unclear; but it would appear that mechanisms are in place based on information on China's website.

Table 7: Codex Alimentarius Commission

Products	Definition	Legislation/ Regulations/Guidelines	Regulatory Agency	Marketing Authorization
Vitamins and Mineral food supplements	For the purpose of the Codex Guidelines for Vitamins and Mineral Food Supplements, vitamin and mineral food supplements are defined as deriving their nutritional relevance primarily from the minerals and/or vitamins they contain. Vitamin and mineral supplements are sources in concentrated forms of those nutrients alone or in combination, marketed in forms such as capsules, tablets, powders, solutions, etc., not in conventional food form and whose purpose is to supplement the intake of vitamins and/or minerals from the normal diet. Food is defined as "any substance, whether processed, semi-processed or raw, which is intended for human consumption, and includes drink, chewing gum, and any substance which has been used in the manufacture, preparation or treatment of food but does not include cosmetics or tobacco or substances used only as drugs".	Codex was created in 1963 by Food & Agriculture Organization of the United Nations and WHO to develop food standards, guidelines and related texts such as codes of practice. Codex Proposed Draft Guidelines for Vitamins and Mineral Food Supplements. These guidelines apply in those jurisdictions where vitamin and mineral food supplement products are regulated as foods. The classification of these vitamin and mineral supplements is left to national regulations.	Codex Committee on Nutrition and Foods for Special Dietary Uses. Codex Alimentarius Commission , Joint FAO/WHO Food Standards Programme.	N/A

Table 8: European Union (Overview)

Products	Definition	Legislation/ Regulations/ Guidelines	Regulatory Agency	Marketing Authorization
Herbal Products	Medical product-Any substance or combination of substances which may be administered to human beings to make a medical diagnosis or to restore, correct or modify physiological functions in humans. Substance is any matter of the following origin: human, animal (including microorganisms, organs, secretions, parts, extractions). vegetable (including microorganisms, plants, plant parts, extracts, secretions) and chemical. Traditional Herbal Medicine was defined differently in the proposed Directive and has been now retracted.	Directive 2001/83; 2003/63 Annex I, Part 3, Chapter 4.	The Agency in the Member State.	In Member State after review of documentation (monograph) by Local Committee. Approval for five years with renewal.
Vitamins and Minerals	Same as herbal products , when in medicinal strength/medicinal product	Directive 2001/83.	Agency in Member State	Review by State Committee.
Food Supplements	Supplements that are pre-packaged and marketed as foods. Foodstuffs in concentrated form to supplement the normal diet & having nutritional or physiological effects (Vitamins and Minerals).	Directive 2002/46	Standing Committee on Food Chain and Animal Health regulates the level of vitamins & minerals.	National Restrictions and allowances apply. Maximum daily.
Homeopathics	Any product made from products, substances & compositions called homeopathic stock according to homeopathic pharmacopoeias.	Directive 2001/83 Chapter 2. Directive 2003/63 Annex I, Part III, Chapter 3.	Agency in Member State.	Simplified registration & proof allowed. Member State Committee approval required. Allowance for different rules in Member States.
Fortified Foods	All food containing voluntarily added vitamins & minerals to replace nutritive value lost during processing, to produce substitute foods & to fortify foods.	Vitamins &Minerals in Foods Proposal 2003/0262 COD	Standing Committee on Food Chain and Animal Health regulates the level of vitamins & minerals allowed in food. Fortified foods are included in a register.	Regulation on labeling, advertising and presentation.

Table 9: European Union (Regulatory Components)

Products	Product Licensing/ Registration	Risk/Scientific Assessments/ Standards of Evidence (SOEs)	Site Licensing	Good Manufacturing Practices (GMPs)	Adverse Reaction Reporting
Herbal Products	Yes	Reduced	Member State	Yes	Yes
Vitamins and Minerals	Yes	Yes	Member State	Yes	Yes
Food Supplements	Yes	Yes	Member State	?	?
Homeopathics	Yes	Reduced	Member State	Yes	Yes

Table 10: France (Overview)

Products	Definition	Legislation/ Regulations	Regulatory Agency	Marketing Authorization
Herbal products	All medicinal herbs listed in the European Union pharmacopeia and in the French pharmacopeia. The French pharmacopeia is in addition to the European one.	Public Health Code (PHC) (Code de la Santé Publique) Legislative and Regulatory parts. Herbal medicinal products are regulated as drugs and can only be prepared by pharmacists or qualified herbalists. EU guideline on herbal medicines issued in July 2001 (CPMP/QWP/2820/00).	French Agency for the Safety of Medical Products - Agence française de sécurité sanitaire des produits de santé (AFSSAPS) European Agency for the Evaluation of Medicinal Products (EMEA)	Yes, for all herbal medicinal products. Authorization obtained from AFSSAPS or the European Agency for the Evaluation of Medicinal Products (EMEA)
Vitamins and minerals	Vitamins and minerals are allowed in dietary products and food supplements (with limits for some). JO 12/4/1996.	Public Health Code (PHC) (Code de la Santé Publique) Legislative and regulatory parts.	AFSSAPS EMEA	AFSSAPS EMEA
Food Supplements	The French legislation does not precisely distinguish between what is a drug and what is a supplement. It considers as a drug any substance having properties to cure or prevent human diseases or any product which contains a substance having a therapeutic action. This definition then includes herbs, minerals, vitamins, food supplements and dietary supplements as well as drugs.	Public Health Code (PHC) (Code de la Santé Publique) Legislative and regulatory parts.	French Agency for the Safety of Medical Products. - Agence française de sécurité sanitaire des produits de santé (AFSSAPS)	Yes, from AFSSAPS
Homeopathics	Any medication obtained from products, substances or compositions called source substances, through an homeopathic manufacturing process described in the European pharmacopeia, the French pharmacopeia or, if not available, in the pharmacopeia officially utilized in another member state of the European Community.	Public Health Code (PHC) (Code de la Santé Publique) Legislative and regulatory parts. Article L.511-1	French Agency for the Safety of Medical Products. - Agence française de sécurité sanitaire des produits de santé (AFSSAPS)	Yes : except for those that are administered orally or externally, for which no therapeutic claim is made and are sufficiently diluted to ensure their safety. (Directives 92/73/EEC, 92/74/EEC and PHC L.512l-13)

Table 11:   France (Regulatory Components)

Products	Product Licensing/ Registration	Risk/Scientific Assessments	Site Licensing	Good Manufacturing Practices	Adverse Reaction Reporting
Herbal Products	Yes. All herbal products covered by the legislation must be registered with AFSSAPS.	Herbal products are not required to go through the same rigorous scientific assessments as other drugs. French Food Safety Agency - Agence française de sécurité sanitaire des aliments (AFSSA)	AFSSAPS European Agency for the Evaluation of Medicinal Products (EMEA)	Yes. Their production must follow the process described in the recognized pharmacopoeias. (Directive 2003/94/ EC and PHC L5121-6). Enforced by AFSSAPS and the European Agency for the Evaluation of Medicinal Products (EMEA):	Yes. Physicians, pharmacists, manufacturers or other health professionals must report adverse reactions to AFSSAPS.
Vitamins and Minerals	Yes, if amount sufficiently high enough to be considered as medical products. Directive. Also as per Directive 2002/46/EC.	French Food Safety Agency (AFSSA)	Yes if medical product	Yes	Yes if medical product
Food Supplements	Yes, as per Directive 2002/46/ EC.Otherwise must conform to Public Health Code to the French food laws.	French Food Safety Agency (AFSSA)	Yes if considered medical product. If not, must conform to European and French food laws.	Yes	Yes, if medical product.
Homeopathics	Yes. All homeopathic products must be registered with AFSSAPS	French Food Safety Agency - Agence française de sécurité sanitaire des aliments (AFSSA)	Yes.	Yes	Yes

Table 12:   Germany (Overview)

Products	Definition	Legislation/ Regulations	Regulatory Agency	Marketing Authorization
Herbal products	All substances designed to treat, heal, sooth or prevent disease or injury in humans and animals.	Arznei Mittel Gezetz 1976 with updates. (AMG 1976); EC Directive 2003/93.	Bundes Ministerium fur Gesundheit and Sociale Sicherheit (Federal Ministry for Health and Social Services)	Federal Authorization after review of Monograph by Commission E; Can be sold outside a pharmacy.
Vitamins and minerals	All substances designed to treat, heal, sooth or prevent disease or injury in humans and animals.	Listed as Medicine under Arznei Mittel Gezetz 1976 with updates. (AMG 1976); EC Directive 2003/93.	Bundes Ministerium fur Gesundheit and Sociale Sicherheit (Federal Ministry for Health and Social Services)	Federal Authorization. Only sold through Pharmacies. Jurisprudence shows that products with strength > 3RDA only sold through pharmacies.
Food Supplements	All substances designed to treat, heal, sooth or prevent disease or injury in humans and animals.	Arznei Mittel Gezetz 1976 with updates. (AMG 1976); EC Directive 2003/93.	Bundes Ministerium fur Gesundheit and Sociale Sicherheit (Federal Ministry for Health and Social Services)	Federal Authorization after Review by respective Commissions.
Homeopathics	All medicine registered in the Homeopathic Medicine Register.	AMG 1976. (Legal codex: Homöopathisches Arzneibuch, the German homeopathic pharmacopoeia.)	Bundes Ministerium fur Gesundheit and Sociale Sicherheit (Federal Ministry for Health and Social Services)	Federal Authorization re: the inclusion in the Homeopathic Medicine Register after review by Homeopathy Commission. Only sold through Pharmacies.
Fortified Foods	Foods supplemented with vitamins, amino acids, minerals and others.	Inclusion of vitamins in food is regulated by the Food Act (LMG 1974). Allows Vitamin A & D in food. Other Regulation is the Vitamin-Verordnung 1942, describing Vitamins C, B1, B2, B6, Phanthetonate, Vitamin E & Niacin & some minerals. Law cites that without regulation vitamins can be added up to 3 times the RDA. Discussions on amount to be allowed will follow proposed EU regulation 2003/0262.	Bundes Ministerium fur Verbraucherschutz, Erharung und Landwirtschaft (Federal Ministry for Consumer protection, Nutrition and Agriculture).	Registered with the Ministry of Foods, and listed in the "Food Book".

Table 13:   Germany (Regulatory Components)

Products	Product Licensing/ Registration	Risk/Scientific Assessments/ Standards of Evidence	Site Licensing	Good Manufacturing Practices	Adverse Reaction Reporting
Herbal Products	Yes	Centrally by Ministry, all documentation deposited with the Deutschen Institut für Medizinische Documentation. All data included in Arznei Buch; Review by Commission E (until 1994 Commission E prepared the monographs), herbals; Commission C Anthroposophic medicine; and Commission 109a AMG 76, Traditional Medicine.	Yes, by the local governments	Yes	Centrally by Ministry, all documentation deposited with the Deutschen Institut für Medizinische Documentation
Vitamins and Minerals	Yes	Same	Same		Same
Food Supplements	Yes	Same	Same		Same
Homeopathics	Yes	Same. Review only by Commission D homeopathic.	Same		Same

Table 14:   Hong Kong (Overview)

Products	Definition	Legislation/ Regulations/Guidelines	Regulatory Agency	Marketing Authorization
Chinese Herbal Medicine (Herbs)	These are defined by two herbal schedules one for potent herbs for prescription use only, and another that lists 574 commonly used herbs (OTC).	The Chinese Medicine Ordinance (Cap. 549) was passed by Legislative Council on July 14, 1999. Subsidiary legislation on Chinese medicines was passed by the Legislative Council in Jan. 2003. This Ordinance was derived from the Article 138 of the Basic Law of the Hong Kong Special Administrative Region Government. Guidelines exist for various topics such as renewal of Chinese Medicine Traders licenses, Retailers and Wholesalers of Chinese herbal medicines.	The Chinese Medicine Council of Hong Kong was established in Sept. 1999 and it is the statutory body to implement the regulatory system.	Not applicable.
Proprietary Chinese Medicines	Any proprietary product composed solely of the following as active ingredients: (i)any Chinese herbal medicine; or (ii)any materials of herbal, animal or mineral origin customarily used by the Chinese; or any medicines and materials referred to in (i) or (ii). They are formulated in a finished dose form and known or claimed to be used for the diagnosis, treatment, prevention or alleviation of any disease or any symptom of a disease in human beings, or for the regulation of the functional states of the human body.	Same as above. Registration of proprietary Chinese medicines began in December 2003. Guidelines exist for Good Manufacturing Practices, Renewal of licenses, and a Handbook exists for the Registration of Proprietary Chinese medicines (56 pages).	Same as above.	Yes; a registration system is used that focuses on safety, quality and efficacy.

Table 15: Hong Kong (Regulatory Components)

Products	Product Licensing/Registration	Risk/Scientific Assessment/Standards of Evidence (SOEs)	Site Licensing	Good Manufacturing Practices (GMPs)	Adverse Reaction Reporting
Chinese Herbal Medicine (Herbs)	Not Applicable.	Use of two schedules: one for potent herbs and a second for 574 commonly used herbs. Prescriptions of Chinese medicine practitioners for potent herbs. Can make claims to have general beneficial effects on health.	Licensing of importers and wholesalers of herbs. Licensing of retailers of herbs. Good Agricultural Practices are applicable.	Standardization of processing methods. Standards of processed herbs.	Guidelines under development.
Proprietary Chinese Medicines (pCm's)	Yes: a registration system is used that focuses on safety, quality and efficacy. Three categories: well-established drugs, new drugs and health products.	Registration system is based on safety, quality and efficacy. Can make claims to prevent or cure a specific disease or clinical condition substantiated with a clinical trial and medicinal test results.	Licensing of manufacturers. licensing of importers and wholesalers. Good Agricultural Practices are applicable.	Yes for manufacturers of pCm's.	Compulsory post-marketing adverse reaction reporting system. Guidelines under development.

Table 16: India (Overview)

Products	Definition	Legislation/Regulations	Regulatory Agency	Marketing Authorization
Herbal products	Herbal products identified as Ayurvedic drugs in the Drug and Cosmetics Act	Drug and Cosmetics Act 1940 and Rules 1945.	Drugs Controller in each State government.	Yes. All medicinal products must be licensed to be sold and distributed.
Vitamins and minerals	Regulated as food supplements.	Drug and Cosmetics Act 1940 and Rules 1945 if considered as medicine and under the Prevention of Food Adulteration Act if considered as food.	Drugs Controller in each State government.	Yes if under the Drugs and Cosmetics Act
Food Supplements	Food supplement can be registered as food or as medicine.	Food supplements come under the Drugs and Cosmetics Act if considered as medicine and under the Prevention of Food Adulteration Act if considered as food.	Drugs Controller in each State government.	Yes if under the Drugs and Cosmetics Act
Homoeopathics	Homoeopathic medicines are covered under the provisions of Drugs & Cosmetic Act 1940 and the Rules made there under.	The manufacture and sale of Homoeopathic drugs is regulated under the provisions of the Drug and Cosmetic Act 1940 and Rules 1945.	State governments.	Yes

Table 17:   India (Regulatory Components)

Products	Product Licensing/ Registration	Risk/Scientific Assessments	Site Licensing	Good Manufacturing Practices	Adverse Reaction Reporting
Herbal Products	Yes, Drugs and Cosmetics Act	None found.	Yes, Drug and Cosmetics Act	Yes. Standards of the Ayurvedic and Unani pharmacopoeas are to be followed. Should also follow Good Manufacturing Practices as per Schedule M of the Drugs and Cosmetics Act.	India does not have a mandatory system for adverse reaction reporting.
Vitamins and Minerals	See Note				
Food Supplements	Yes, if under the Drugs and Cosmetics Act or the Prevention of Food Adulteration Act.	Yes, if under the Drugs and Cosmetics Act or the Prevention of Food Adulteration Act.	Yes, if under the Drugs and Cosmetics Act or the Prevention of Food Adulteration Act.	Yes, if under the Drugs and Cosmetics Act or the Prevention of Food Adulteration Act.	Yes, if under the Drugs and Cosmetics Act or the Prevention of Food Adulteration Act.
Homoeopathics	Yes, Drugs and Cosmetics Act	Yes	Yes	Yes. Standards provided in the homeopathic pharmacopoeia are expected to be followed	India does not have a mandatory system for adverse reaction reporting

Note: No specific information was found on regulations concerning vitamins and minerals production in India.

Table 18:   United Kingdom (Overview)

Products	Definition	Legislation/ Regulations	Regulatory Agency	Marketing Authorization
Herbal products	"... a medicinal product consisting of a substance produced by subjecting a plant or plants to drying, crushing or any other process, or of a mixture whose sole ingredients are two or more substances so produced, or of a mixture whose sole ingredients are one or more substances so produced and water or some other inert substance." Section 132, Medicines Act.	Medicines Act 1968, Section 12(1) Herbal remedies that are industrially produced are regulated as drugs.	Medicines and Healthcare Products Regulatory Agency	At present, the majority of herbal medicines on the UK market are sold and supplied as unlicensed herbal remedies under a legal provision dating back to 1968. However, all herbal medicines that are industrially produced must be licensed.
Vitamins and minerals	Directive 2002/46/EC contains a list of vitamins and minerals that can be used in food supplements	Vitamin and mineral supplements regulated as foods are subject to the general provisions of food law, including the Food Safety Act 1990 and the Food Labelling Regulations 1996.	Food Standards Agency	No
Food Supplements	Defined in "The Food Supplements (England) Regulations 2003"	Supplements (England) Regulations 2003. These regulations implement Directive 2003/46/EC in England effective August 1, 2005	Food Standards Agency	No
Homeopathics	As per Article 1, Directive 92/73EEC, "Any medicinal product prepared from products, substances or composition called homoeopathic stocks in accordance with a homoeopathic manufacturing procedure described by the European Pharmacopoeia or, in the absence thereof, by the pharmacopoeias currently used officially in the Member States".	Medicines Act 1968	Medicines and Healthcare Products Regulatory Agency	If a homeopathic medicinal product is to be marketed in the UK under the registration scheme, a registration certificate must be held by the person responsible for placing it on the market.

79

Table 19:   United Kingdom (Regulatory Components)

Products	Product Licensing/Registration	Risk/Scientific Assessments	Site Licensing	Good Manufacturing Practices (GMP)	Adverse Reaction Reporting
Herbal Products	Yes, for industrially manufactured products.	Yes, for industrially manufactured products.	Medicinal products manufactured in the UK must be produced on a site that holds an appropriate manufacturer's license.	Industrially produced herbal medicinal products are subject to the same good manufacturing practices as all other medicinal products. Exempt herbal remedies are not covered by the GMP regulations. Directive 91/356/EEC.	Yes. Doctors, pharmacists and nurses are asked to report any suspected adverse reaction to any herbal remedies.
Vitamins and Minerals	Directive 2002/46/EC covers the amount of vitamins and minerals that can be included in food supplements. It also establishes a framework for setting maximum levels for vitamins and minerals in food supplements.	No, unless considered as medical products	No, unless considered as medical products	No but product must be prepared and package in accordance with the Food Supplements (England) Regulations.	No
Food Supplements	Directive 2002/46/EC	No unless considered as medical products	No	No unless considered a medical product	No
Homeopathics	As per European Directive 92/73 EEC for products new to the UK market	Applications referred to the Advisory Board on the Registration of Homoeopathic Products (ABRHP)	A company which manufactures, or which proposes to manufacture, homoeopathic medicinal products will need a *manufacturer's license.*	Yes, as per Directive 91/356/EEC which sets out the principles and guidelines of Good Manufacturing Practice for medicinal products.	Yes. Doctors, pharmacists and nurses are asked to report any suspected adverse reaction to any herbal remedies.

Table 20:   USA (Overview-DSHEA)

Products	Definition	Legislation/ Regulations/ Guidelines	Regulatory Agency	Marketing Authorization
Dietary Supplements: a general term to describe a variety of health products.	A dietary supplement (DS) is defined as a product (other than tobacco) taken by mouth that contains a "dietary ingredient" (DI) intended to supplement the diet. The DIs in these products may include: herbs or other botanical, vitamins, minerals, amino acids and a dietary substance for use by man to supplement the diet by increasing the total dietary intake; or a concentrate, metabolite, constituent, extract or combination of any of the above ingredients. A "new DI" is one that contains one (or a combination) of the above ingredients and was not sold in the US in a DS prior to Oct. 15, 1994.	FDA regulates dietary supplements under a different set of regulations (DSHEA) than those covering "conventional" foods and drug products (prescription & OTC). DS are regulated under the Dietary Supplement Health and Education Act of 1994 (DSHEA) which amended Section 201of the Federal Food, Drug and Cosmetic Act with 21 U.S.C. 321 (ff). The US currently has 8 bills in congress on DS: these range from increasing DS safety to more funding for enforcement. The FDA has proposed DS regulations in labelling and claims; Current Good Manufacturing Practices; New Dietary Ingredients and 7 Guidance documents	Center for Food Safety and Applied Nutrition, US Food and Drug Administration, US Department of Health and Human Services.	Dietary supplements do not need approval from the FDA before they are marketed and therefore they are not licensed. One exception is in the case of a "new dietary ingredient", where pre-market review for safety data and other information is required by law.
Fortified Food	Food additives such as vitamins or minerals.	FDA regulates through food standards and food additive regulations. These control what nutrients can be added to food. Substitute foods must be nutritionally equivalent to food replaced or food must be labeled "imitation".	Center for Food Safety and Applied Nutrition, Office of Food Additive Safety, US Food and Drug Administration, US Department of Health and Human Services.	Assessment needed to obtain pre-market approval for food additives.

Table 21:   USA (DSHEA- Regulatory Components)

Products	Product Licensing/ Registration	Risk/Scientific Assessments/ Standards of Evidence (SOE's)	Site Licensing	Good Manufacturing Practices (GMP's)	Adverse Reaction Reporting
A dietary supplement (DS) is defined as a product taken by mouth that contains a "dietary ingredient"(DI) intended to supplement the diet. The DIs in these products may include: herbs or other botanical, vitamins, minerals, an amino acid and a dietary substance for use by man to supplement the diet by increasing the total dietary intake; or a concentrate, metabolite, constituent, extract or combination of any of the above ingredients.	Dietary supplements do not need approval from the FDA before they are marketed and therefore they are not licensed. The one exception is in the case of a "new dietary ingredient", where pre-market review for safety data and other information is required by law. DSHEA restricts nutritional support claims made on DS labels to descriptions of "the role of a nutrient or dietary ingredient intended to affect the structure or function in humans" or "the documented mechanism by which the supplement acts to maintain such structure or function." An FDA disclaimer is required on DS, stating that the FDA has not evaluated it & the product is not intended to diagnose, treat, cure, or prevent any disease.	A DS manufacturer is responsible for ensuring that a DS is safe before it is marketed. FDA is responsible for taking action against any unsafe DS product after it is on the market. DSHEA lists 4 reasons that a DS could be classified as adulterated; it would be then subject to FDA regulation; these reasons are: 1) the DS poses a "significant or unreasonable risk of illness or injury" when used according to label directions; 2) the DS contains a new ingredient that cannot be shown to be safe; 3) the Secretary declares the DS poses an "imminent hazard to public health or safety"; or 4) the DS contains "poisonous or unsanitary" ingredients pursuant to Food, Drug & Cosmetic Act	No: Manufacturers do not need to register themselves nor their dietary supplement products with FDA before producing or selling them.	Yes: DS products are required to be prepared, packaged, and stored in accordance with Current Good Manufacturing Practices applicable to food products. All ingredients must be truthfully and accurately listed on the label and the product may not be adulterated with other substances. The FDA has recently proposed (May 6, 2003) DS regulations in Current Good Manufacturing Practices. These will not impose standards for which there is no current and generally available analytical methodology.	Reporting adverse reactions is voluntary and carries no legal obligations. The FDA enters & analyses all reports of adverse events they receive into the Center for Food Safety and Applied Nutrition's Special Nutritionals Adverse Event Monitoring System. The FDA also uses its MedWatch system to track serious events. The FDA receives passive surveillance data on adverse events associated with food and DS through the Drug Quality Reporting System and the Office of regulatory Affairs Consumer Complaint System.

APPENDIX 1:

LIST OF NATIONAL WEB SITES FOR COUNTRIES THAT REGULATE NATURAL HEALTH PRODUCTS

1. **Australia**
   Their definition of complementary medicines incorporates what Canada defines as natural health products. Their Therapeutic Goods Administration web site is:
   http://www.health.gov.au/tga/
2. **China**
   Their State Food and Drug Administration is their federal regulator. Their web site is only in Chinese and it is located at: *http://www.sda.gov.cn/webportal/portal.po*
3. **Codex Alimentarius**
   Codex is mandated to set international standards for trade in all types of food products. The web site is:
   http://www.codexalimentarius.net/.
4. **European Commission**
   A useful web site for legislation is located at:
   http://pharmacos.eudra.org/F2/home.html
5. **France**
   Their French Health Products Safety Agency covers the herbal and homeopathic drugs and their web site is at:
   http://agmed.sante.gouv.fr/

6. **Germany**
   Their federal web site that would cover herbal and homeopathic drugs is located at:
   http://www.bfarm.de/de/index.php

7. **India**
   Their regulations cover Indian herbal and homeopathic medicines and the main organization is the Central Drugs Standard Control Organization and their web site is at:
   http://www.cdsco.nic.in/

8. **Hong Kong**
   The Chinese Medical Council of Hong Kong is the regulator of herbal medicines in Hong Kong under the Chinese Medicines Ordinance and the Chinese Medicines Regulations. Their web site is located at:
   http://www.cmchk.org.hk/pcm/eng/idx_news.htm

9. **USA**
   In the United States the main internet portal is the following: *http://www.fda.gov/oc/industry/default.htm* and homeopathic drugs are covered under the Federal Food, Drug and Cosmetics Act. Most of the health products such as vitamins, minerals, herbs and supplements are covered by the Dietary Supplement Health and Education Act of 1994 and their web site is located at:
   http://www.cfsan.fda.gov/~dms/supplmnt.html.
   Under the Dietary Supplement Health and Education Act of 1994 (DSHEA), the dietary supplement manufacturer is responsible for ensuring that a dietary supplement is safe before it is marketed. FDA is responsible for taking action against any unsafe dietary supplement product after it reaches the market. Generally, manufacturers do not need to register with FDA nor get FDA approval before producing or selling dietary supplements. Manufacturers must make sure that product label information is truthful and not misleading.

10. **UK**
    In the UK the Medicines and Healthcare products Regulatory Agency is located at:
    http://www.mhra.gov.uk/.

11. World Health Organization

The WHO group covering Traditional Medicines is to be found at:

http://www.who.int/medicines/organization/trm/orgtrmmain1. shtml.

The WHO Policy and Strategy on Traditional Medicine is located at:

http://www.who.int/medicines/organization/trm/orgtrmmain. shtml.

Appendix 2

Australia

1.0   Australian Law

In Australia, the components of legislation are divided into:
1. Acts;
2. Statutory Rules including Regulations; and
3. Explanatory Statements of Statutory Rules (Amendments).

The Australian national legislation, including the Australian Therapeutic Goods Act 1989, is set out at *http://www.scaleplus.law.gov.au/browse.htm*. Guidelines for the regulations are sets of information for the detailed interpretation of regulations and, in the case of the Australian Regulatory Guidelines for Complementary Medicines, a set is found at *http://www.health.gov.au/tga/cm.htm* . Most of the material listed below in sections 2.0 to 8.0 was derived from the Australian web sites listed above which cover the Australian Therapeutic Goods Act 1989.

2.0   The Regulatory Framework
for Complementary Medicines in Australia

The *Australian Therapeutic Goods Act 1989* came into effect in February 1991 and is designed to provide a national system of controls over the quality, safety, efficacy and timely availability of imported or locally manufactured therapeutic goods used in Australia and/ or exported from Australia. It applies to matters relating to trade or commerce between Australia and other countries, and between States and Territories within Australia.

The Therapeutic Goods Administration (TGA), an administrative body within the Australian Department of Human Services and Health, is charged with administering the Act. "Complementary therapies" include a diverse group of health-related therapies and disciplines that are not considered to be a part of mainstream medical care in Australia. Their web site is : *http://www,health.gov.au/tga/* . Material was taken from the TGA web site for this report and modified to describe their systems, processes and their latest initiatives.

The different types of complementary medicines in the Australian regulatory framework are:
1. Registered Prescription Medicines;
2. Registered non-Prescription Medicines;
3. Listed Medicines; and
4. Complementary medicines.

3.0   COMPLEMENTARY MEDICINES: REGULATORY DEFINITION

"Complementary medicines" include herbal medicines, vitamin and mineral supplements, other nutritional supplements, traditional medicines such as Ayurvedic medicines and traditional Chinese medicines (TCM), homoeopathic medicines, and aromatherapy oils.

The Therapeutic Goods Administration maintains the Australian Register of Therapeutic Goods (ARTG). The ARTG includes details of all therapeutic goods that are imported into, supplied in, or exported from Australia. It is a legal requirement that, unless specifically exempt or excluded, all therapeutic goods must be included in the ARTG before their importation, exportation, manufacture, or supply. In general, only therapeutic goods that have been assessed or evaluated by the TGA are included in the ARTG. There are approximately 16,000 complementary medicines included in the ARTG.

For the purpose of regulating complementary medicines, the *Therapeutic Goods Act 1989* (Section 52F, Definitions; Commonwealth of Australia, *Therapeutic Goods Regulations 1990* as amended) and the *Therapeutic Goods Regulations* (the Regulations) respectively define what is a complementary medicine and designate the types of active ingredients that may be used in such medicines. The objective of the Regulations is to prescribe in matters in respect of the manufacture, supply, advertising, registering or listing of medicines so as to make it necessary or convenient to carry out or give effect to the Act. A complementary medicine is defined as a therapeutic good consisting wholly or principally of one or more designated active ingredients (the Regulations: Schedule 14, Designated active ingredients), each of which has a clearly established identity and a traditional use.

Traditional use means use of the designated active ingredient that is well documented, or otherwise established, according to the accumulated experience of many traditional healthcare practitioners over an extended period of time. It accords with well-established procedures of preparation, application and dosage. Medicines not meeting the definition cannot be regulated as complementary medicines.

Complementary medicines may be included on the ARTG as Listed or Registered medicines. Registered complementary medicines may be non-prescription, over-the-counter (OTC) medicines or medicines available only on prescription from a medical practitioner or other authorized prescriber registered under a law of a State or Territory.

4.0   COMPLEMENTARY MEDICINES: QUALITY, SAFETY AND EFFICACY

In supporting the overall objective of the Act to ensure the quality, safety, efficacy, and timely availability of therapeutic goods supplied in or exported from Australia, the TGA's regulatory processes include three key elements: pre-market assessment of products, the licensing and audit of manufacturers, and a range of post-market activities including adverse reaction reporting.

4.1   PRE-MARKET ASSESSMENT

Important developments in the pre-market assessment process in the TGA's regulatory system for complementary medicines were based on a regulatory reform package introduced into legislation in 1999. The reforms, among other things, applied a risk-based approach to determine appropriate standards for pre-market assessment and evaluation (and post-market activities). The pre-market assessment procedure undertaken by the TGA is determined by risk. In determining risk and the evaluation process to be applied, a number of factors are taken into consideration. These factors include: the toxicity of the ingredients (itself a complex of factors); whether the medicine is indicated for a serious form of a disease, condition or disorder, or for the treatment, cure, management or prevention of a disease, condition or disorder; whether the use of the medicine is likely to result in significant side effects, including interactions with other medicines; and whether there may be adverse effects from prolonged use or inappropriate self-medication.

Based on risk, the TGA has a two-tiered approach to regulation of therapeutic goods. Medicines that are assessed to be of higher risk on the medicines risk continuum, are individually evaluated for quality, safety and efficacy. If, following evaluation, they are approved by the TGA for supply, the products are included in the ARTG as Registered medicines. Efficacy is usually assessed by examining data from controlled clinical trials. Registered medicines include both prescription and non-prescription medicines.

Listed medicines are of lower risk than Registered medicines. Most complementary medicines included in the ARTG are Listed medicines. There are approximately 15,200 Listed complementary medicines and approximately 800 Registered complementary medicines included in the ARTG. Listed and Registered medicines can be differentiated on the product label by the designation, respectively, of AUST L or AUST R followed by a unique number.

The assessment of Listed medicines, their inclusion in the ARTG, the evaluation of quality and safety of new complementary medicine ingredients for use in their inclusion in the ARTG, is managed within the TGA by the Office of Complementary Medicines (OCM). Listed (low risk) complementary medicines are included in the ARTG via a simple, low-cost and streamlined electronic application process. Listed medicines are low risk because they may contain only ingredients that have been evaluated by the TGA to be low risk, they must be manufactured by licensed manufacturers in accordance with the principles of GMP and they may carry indications only for health maintenance and health enhancement or certain indications for non-serious, self-limiting conditions. Listed medicines may not refer to serious forms of disease, disorders or conditions and, generally, must not indicate that they are for treatment, cure, management or prevention of disease, disorders or conditions.

The Listing Process

In contrast to the evaluation process for Registered medicines, Listed medicines may be supplied following application to the TGA by the sponsor of the product and self-certification, and validation by the TGA that certain key requirements of the legislation are being met. A sponsor of a therapeutic good is the person or company responsible for applying to the TGA to have their goods included on the ARTG. The sponsor must be a resident of Australia or carrying on business in Australia.

Listed medicines are not individually evaluated by the TGA before they are released onto the market. Product details are required by a sponsor who submits an application to the TGA to include a medicine on the ARTG as a Listed medicine. At the time of submitting a Listing application to the TGA, the sponsor certifies that the goods that are the subject of the application meet the requirements of Section 26A(2) (a)B(k) inclusive and, if applicable, subsection 26A(3) of the Act. In certifying under Section 26A(2) (a)B(k) of the Act, the sponsor makes a legally binding statement that:

a) the medicine is eligible for listing;
b) the medicine is safe for the purposes for which it is to be used;
c) the medicine presentation is not unacceptable, and the medicine conforms to every standard (if any) applicable to the medicine and to every requirement (if any) relating to advertising applicable under the Regulations;
d) for medicines manufactured in Australia, each step has been carried out by a person who is the holder of a licence to carry out that step (before a sponsor uses an overseas manufacturer, they are required to seek pre-clearance by the TGA that the manufacturer is of an acceptable standard);
e) the medicine complies with all prescribed quality or safety criteria;
f) the medicine does not contain substances that are prohibited imports for the purposes of the *Customs Act 1901(Customs Act 1901* as amended*)*;
g) the applicant holds information or evidence to support any claim that the applicant makes relating to the medicine; and
h) the information included in, or with, the application is correct.

Ingredients Permitted in Listed Medicines

Listed medicines may be supplied only if they contain active ingredients permitted under Schedule 4 of the Regulations (Commonwealth of Australia, Schedule 4, Therapeutic Goods Regulations 1990 as amended). Schedule 4 (Part 1, Item 3) outlines those goods that must be included in the part of the ARTG for Listed goods. These include preparations containing as their therapeutically active ingredients only vitamins, minerals, herbal substances or other substances specified in Part 5 of this Schedule, or a combination of those substances where:

a) the preparation:
   (i) is not included in a Schedule to the Poisons Standard; and
   (ii) is not of a kind required to be sterile; and
b) the vitamins consist only of vitamins or their salts specified in Part 2 of this Schedule; and
c) the minerals consist only of minerals or their salts specified in Part 3 of this Schedule; and
d) the herbal substances are not included in Part 4 of this Schedule; and
e) the herbal substance is present in therapeutic goods included in the ARTG for supply in Australia;
f) if a substance mentioned in Division 2 of Part 5 is an ingredient - the preparation is not supplied:
   (i) in a form that contains the substance in excess of the maximum amount per dosage for that form as mentioned in column 2 of the table in that Division for that substance; and
   (ii) without the information about daily dosage mentioned in column 3 of the table for that substance;
   (iii) unless the indications proposed by the sponsor of the preparation are in the treatment of a condition referred to in clause 4 of the Therapeutic Goods Advertising Code.

With the exception of herbal ingredients, Schedule 4 of the Regulations includes lists of ingredients that may be included in Listed medicines. In the case of herbal ingredients, any herbal ingredient that is currently included in a therapeutic good included in the ARTG may be used in Listed medicines unless it is included in a Schedule or otherwise restricted in the Standard for the Uniform Scheduling of Drugs and Poisons (SUSDP) (the Poisons standard), or included in Part 4 of Schedule 4 or otherwise restricted by Part 5 (Division 2) of the Regulations. A consolidated list of substances that may be used as active ingredients in Listed medicines, including herbal substances, is available on the TGA's website *www.tga.gov.au/docs/html/ listsubs.htm* .

The majority of substances that can be included in Listed medicines are those that were included in therapeutic goods supplied in Australia before the Act came into operation in 1991. These goods were included in the ARTG with little assessment ("grandfathered").

However, as part of the "grandfathered" process and subsequent on-going review, some herbal substances were not considered to be low risk and were excluded from use in Listed medicines.

Listed Medicines: Special Consideration of Herbal Ingredients

Herbal substances can be found in a wide range of complementary medicines. They comprise the active ingredients in herbal medicines formulated according to European, Chinese, Ayurvedic and other traditions. Herbal ingredients are also often included in vitamin and mineral supplements, sun screens (as excipients) and registered medicines. An "excipient" is an ingredient of a medicine other than an active ingredient.

Herbal ingredients are chemically complex and contain a wide range of chemical components. Typically, herbal preparations consist of active components, secondary components, and accompanying compounds. For most herbs, the active components have not been identified or verified. These components differ in their biological activity, adverse effects and interactions with each other. The biological activity of herbal preparations may result from additive, synergistic or antagonistic effects of their components. Plant components that may not be active themselves may affect the stability, solubility, and bioavailability of the active component(s). Herbal components may also differ in the extent to which they are soluble in extraction solvents such as water and alcohol. The use of non-traditional methods of preparation, including use of non-traditional solvents, can quantitatively and/or qualitatively change the component profile. Such a change may affect both the safety and the therapeutic profile of the preparation.

The current regulatory system permits Listed medicines to contain a wide range of herbal ingredients and preparations. Part of determining the eligibility of a herbal substance for use as an ingredient in Listed medicines is whether the substance meets the definition of a "herbal substance" as prescribed in the Regulations.

Herbal Substance: Regulatory Definition

The TGA's Approved Terminology for Medicines (Therapeutic Goods Administration, 1999) classifies herbal ingredients as "herbal substances". Herbal substances are preparations of plants and other organisms, such as fungi and blueBgreen algae, that are treated as plants in the International Code of Botanical Nomenclature (*http:// www.bgbm.fu-berlin.de/iapt/nomenclature/code/Saint*Louis/0000St.Luis-

93

title.htm).

The definition of "herbal substance" in the Regulations includes details of acceptable production processes. Processes not specifically included in the definition (for example, fermentation) are not acceptable, without pre-market evaluation, for producing a herbal substance for use in Listed medicines.

The definition effectively describes the types of herbal ingredients that can be included in Listed medicines in the ARTG. In a regulatory context, "herbal substance" is referred to in Schedule 4 of the Regulations, which describes those therapeutic goods that must be included in the part of the ARTG for Listed goods, and is defined in the Regulations (Regulation 2, Interpretation):

"'Herbal substance' means all or part of a plant or substance (other than a pure chemical or a substance of bacterial origin):
a) that is obtained only by drying, crushing, distilling, extracting, expressing, comminuting, mixing with an inert diluent substance or another herbal substance or mixing with water, ethanol, glycerol or aqueous ethanol; and
b) that is not subjected to any other treatment or process other than a treatment that is necessary for its presentation in pharmaceutical form."

The above definition of herbal substance: excludes preparation methods involving fermentation and/or obtaining selected components through chemical reactions and precipitation; but can include complex multi-step extraction processes using a wide range of solvents provided that these are, in most cases, driven off (water, ethanol and glycerol may remain).

To be considered low risk, a herbal substance must meet the following criteria (Regulations, Schedule 4 Part 1 Item 3):
1. the herbal substance is present in therapeutic goods included in the ARTG for supply in Australia; that is, it must have been previously present in products "approved" for use in Australia; and
2. the preparation must be a herbal substance as defined in the Regulations; and
3. the ingredient, or a component in the ingredient, must not be a poison; that is, included in a Schedule or in Appendix C or Appendix G to the SUSDP; and
4. the ingredient must not have been identified as posing a safety risk and have been included in the Regulations, Schedule

4 Part 4.

Where a herbal ingredient is homoeopathically prepared, separate criteria apply (see Therapeutic Goods Regulations 1990, Schedule 4 Part 1 Items 4A and 5, at www.tga.gov.au/legis/). The first and second criteria refer to previously supplied herbal ingredients and were specified as a practical means of identifying herbal ingredients used in traditional herbal medicine or established pharmaceutical practice as low risk. The third and fourth criteria exclude those substances considered not to be of sufficiently low risk to be suitable for use as ingredients in Listed medicines.

The definition of herbal substance was intended to cover the more usual traditional herbal preparations, such as fresh and dry herbs, essential oils, tinctures, decoctions, infusions and simple extracts. The rationale for this approach was that where there was a history of traditional use or established pharmaceutical practice, herbal medicines prepared and prescribed according to that tradition were likely to be low-risk. On this basis, such substances were considered suitable for use in Listed medicines. If a herbal ingredient, or a component in a herbal ingredient, was considered to cause unacceptable side effects, it was excluded from the low-risk category by the third and fourth criteria, namely by inclusion in the SUSDP or in the *Regulations, Schedule 4, Part 4.*

If evidence based on a history of use has been used to support the safety of a herbal substance, then it is important that any preparation of that substance eligible for use should have a chemical composition equivalent to that used historically. In addition, the dosage, dosage form and route and schedule of administration should also be consistent with that tradition or history. If this is not the case, the ingredient may present a different risk profile to the ingredient used historically. This does not necessarily mean that the substance is unsuitable for use in Listed medicines, but that it should undergo evaluation and approval before being used.

Over recent years, the methods used to process some herbs have moved from traditional to non-traditional. In traditional herbal medicine and established pharmaceutical practice, herbal extracts are usually prepared using water, alcoholic beverages and ethanol as solvents. More recently, non-traditional solvents have been used there may not have been sufficient time to observe the use of novel preparations in a traditional setting to provide the experience to support the safety of these preparations.

It is inappropriate to rely entirely on evidence of a history of use to support the safety of these substances. This issue is broader than that of an ingredient not meeting the definitional requirements of a herbal substance. In fact, many herbal ingredients prepared non-traditionally will meet the definition and potential concerns over their safety need to be addressed.

Evaluation of Ingredients for Use in Listed Complementary Medicines: Process

New ingredients for use in Listed complementary medicines are evaluated by the TGA in response to an application from a sponsor. Based on the data supplied by the sponsor and other data, a comprehensive evaluation report is prepared by the staff of the OCM. The evaluation report is put forward for consideration by the Complementary Medicines Evaluation Committee (CMEC), an independent, expert statutory committee.

Whether a regulatory system is effective, depends to a large extent on its access to professional expertise. The membership of CMEC is broad, to provide the range of expertise required to advise on issues of quality and safety and efficacy in complementary medicines. In addition, the considerations of the CMEC may be supplemented with advice from expert advisers. The CMEC makes recommendations to the TGA about how the ingredient should be regulated, and the TGA makes a regulatory decision based on those recommendations and any other factors deemed relevant. With the range of expertise available to the regulatory system, the TGA has been able to respond appropriately the concerns of consumers, industry and government. Since the inception of the CMEC in 1998, 164 new ingredients for use in Listed complementary medicines have been approved by the TGA. This has given rise to a range of new Listed products containing these ingredients.

The parameters considered when evaluating a complementary medicine substance are quality and safety. Quality aspects are evaluated for the purpose of characterising the substance and establishing a compositional guideline for it. Quality is a critical determinant of the safety of complementary medicines and other medicines. Medicines should be controlled to make sure that they contain the specified ingredients and do not contain unsafe amounts of adulterants, contaminants or active ingredients.

The safety evaluation determines whether the substance, once characterized, is of sufficiently low risk, so as to allow its inclusion as an ingredient in Listed medicines.

Ingredients for Use in Listed Complementary Medicines: Quality

The Act defines the quality standards applicable to all therapeutic goods. For regulatory purposes, the British Pharmacopoeia (BP) is the source of official standards. The BP is supplemented by *Therapeutic Goods Orders (TAOS)*, which are developed by the TGA through a process of industry and other stakeholder consultation in response to a particular need. This may occur where there is no coverage by the BP or where Australian-specific requirements are appropriate. Quality standards for specific products may also be established through the listing/registration process.

Where a new complementary substance is covered by a monograph in the BP, this standard must be applied in its entirety, unless otherwise justified to the TGA. The requirements of applicable general monographs of the BP must also be met, except where a justification for not doing so is authorized by the TGA. The TGA considers the suitability of other national or international pharmacopoeia monographs or standards for the substance on a case-by-case basis. In many instances, there are no applicable monographs, and a compositional guideline must be developed by the sponsor. The TGA is currently developing regulatory guidelines for complementary medicines, including guidance for the quality and safety of complementary medicine substances. This will include criteria for compositional guidelines.

A compositional guideline is a summary of descriptions, tests and limits that defines the composition and relevant characteristics of the substance. Where the pharmacopoeia monograph or standard sufficiently characterises the substance, a separate compositional guideline is not required. It should be noted that a monograph or standard is designed to provide a means of controlling the quality of a substance. It is not intended to characterise the material to the extent required for entry in the ARTG. The compositional guideline should allow for characterisation as well as quality control of the substance.

Compositional guidelines or monographs from other national pharmacopoeias or other standards for complementary medicine substances have no legal basis and, as such, it is not mandatory for sponsors to comply with them.

Ingredients for Use in Listed Complementary Medicines: Safety

The safety of complementary medicine substances for use in Listed medicines is established through an evaluation process that aims to ensure that any substance approved for use in Listed products is of "low risk". Once established as low risk, many complementary medicine substances need no further controls on their use in Listed medicines. However, where risks or potential risks are identified in association with the use or uses of a particular substance (for example, in its use by particular population subgroups, such as children or pregnant women, or in its interactions with other medicines), certain restrictions and/or controls may be imposed to manage the risk, but the substance may still be eligible, with restrictions, for use in Listed medicines.

Such options include the use of label advisory information, restrictions on dosage, route of administration, plant part or plant preparation, and/or restriction of the form in which the substance can be presented. The information and data are normally supplied by the sponsor who is requesting evaluation of the substance. Sometimes substances have been deemed unsuitable by the CMEC for use in Listed medicines, not because of direct evidence of their hazard, but because of insufficient evidence to provide assurance of safety. The criteria used to assess the safety of a complementary medicine substance recognize the need for a level of evaluation commensurate with the level of risk.

In the absence of conventional toxicity data, there are other data for complementary medicine substances that can be used to support the safety evaluation. In evaluating new complementary medicine substances, it is recognized that there may be well-established medicinal, food or other uses of the substance or products containing the substance, that can be used to support or establish safety. Well-established use implies that a sufficient number of people were treated or otherwise exposed to the substance, or to products containing the substance (or substances justified as essentially similar to the substance), over a period of time sufficient to support the safety of the substance for its intended purpose.

The long-term use of some substances may have created a comprehensive body of experience in the published literature. A substance or product containing the substance that has a long history of use is expected to have useful bibliographic data and information published in official pharmacopoeias and scientific reference textbooks. The inclusion of a substance in official pharmacopoeias or reference textbooks may contribute to the substantiation of the substance as a complementary medicine substance (refer to *Section 52F, Definitions, Traditional Use, Therapeutic Goods Act 1989*).

By definition, a complementary medicine substance must have a tradition of use (*Section 52F, Definitions, Traditional Use, Therapeutic Goods Act 1989*). Safety may be established by detailed reference to the published literature, the submission of original study data, or a combination of both. Where there is sufficient evidence based on human experience to support safety, conventional studies involving animal and *in vitro* studies may not be necessary. Where such human experience is deficient, or there are suspicions of effects that are difficult or impossible to detect with confidence in population or in clinical studies, the safety assessment needs to be supported with other studies unless otherwise justified. The absence of reports of untoward effects associated with a particular substance is not assurance that use of a medicine is safe.

Generally, while it is relatively easy to identify substances in a traditional setting that are so hazardous that they produce acute adverse effects in a significant proportion of users, or produce unusual acute effects, it is more difficult to identify adverse effects that develop over a long period, occur infrequently, occur in a small population sub-group, develop from interaction with other medicines or food, or that may be ascribed to an underlying disease or common health problem. If experience of use is deficient, or there is reason to suspect effects that are difficult to detect in a traditional setting or through historical use, safety should be supported by appropriate toxicology studies. The four types of data used to support the safety evaluation of complementary medicine substances for use in Listed medicines are the following:

1. Biological activity: To describe the role of the substance in human metabolism;
2. Toxicology: To describe what is known about and, where possible, quantify, potential risk associated with the use of the substance;
3. Clinical trials: To report the results of use of the substance by humans under clinical trial conditions to identify risks from the experience of use in humans. The TGA does not use the data to evaluate efficacy;
4. Adverse reactions: To determine the nature, severity and frequency of adverse reactions where there has been a history of use of the substance.

Listed Complementary Medicines: Efficacy

Consistent with their low risk, Listed complementary medicines may carry only certain indications and claims for the symptomatic relief of conditions (other than serious disease, disorders, or conditions), health maintenance, health enhancement and risk reduction. Registered complementary medicines may carry higher level claims. Claims on Registered complementary medicines are subject to pre-market evaluation comparable to that undertaken for other medicines of similar risk.

Indications and claims permitted for Listed (low-risk) complementary medicines are the following:

Health maintenance; Health enhancement; Nutritional support; Symptomatic relief of non-serious diseases, disorders and conditions; May aid or assist in the management of non-serious diseases, disorders and conditions; and Reduction in the risk of a particular non-serious disease, disorder, condition, symptom or ailment.

The *Australian Therapeutic Goods Act* requires that, at the time of Listing, sponsors must certify that they hold the evidence to support indications and claims made in relation to listable goods. The indications and claims on Listed medicines are not subject to pre-market evaluation at the time of Listing. The evidence held by sponsors must be sufficient to substantiate that the indications and claims are true, valid and not misleading. To facilitate compliance with the requirement to hold appropriate evidence to support particular claims, the TGA and the CMEC have developed guidelines to assist sponsors in determining the appropriate evidence to support indications and claims made in relation to Listed medicines (*Guidelines for Levels and Kinds of Evidence to Support Indications and Claims* ; see www.tga.gov.au/docs/pdf/tgaccevi.pdf). In particular, the *Guidelines* relate to Listable complementary medicines, sunscreens and other listable medicines.

Registered Complementary Medicines: Evaluation for Quality, Safety and Efficacy

Registered complementary medicines are products that contain an active ingredient that is not permitted for use in Listed medicines or that carry "high level" or otherwise Registerable indications/claims as defined in the Guidelines for Levels and Kinds of Evidence to Support Indications and Claims. Registerable indications/claims are defined as relating to the treatment, management, prevention or cure of diseases or disorders, or which in any other way refer to a serious disease, or treatment of specific named vitamin or mineral deficiency diseases.

Registered complementary medicines are evaluated to the comparable standards of quality, safety and efficacy as required for OTC and prescription medicines, depending on the risk associated with the individual product. Based on the data supplied by the sponsor and other data, a comprehensive evaluation report is prepared by the staff of the OCM.

4.2   LICENSING AND AUDIT OF MANUFACTURERS

The Act requires each Australian manufacturer of medicinal products for human use to hold a manufacturing licence. It is an offence, carrying heavy penalties, to manufacture therapeutic goods without such a licence, unless the goods are exempt from this requirement. Licence holders are required to comply with the manufacturing principles of the Act. These manufacturing principles require compliance with Good Manufacturing Practice (GMP).

A basic principle of GMP is that quality cannot be assured by testing a finished product alone. Testing a finished product for compliance with a regulatory specification is just one component in the quality assurance chain. Regulatory specifications, such as those in a pharmacopoeia monograph, are aimed at selected quality parameters. The specifications are developed on the understanding that the product has been manufactured in accordance with the principles of GMP and in conformity with the TGA-approved formulation. A finished-product specification cannot control for contamination, adulteration or substitution from all possible sources. This is particularly the case for many complementary medicines that may contain chemically complex herbal ingredients and/or multiple ingredients. Australian manufacturers of medicinal products are required to comply with the *Australian Code of GMP for Medicinal Products*.

The Code sets out requirements relating to the following:

Quality management
- This is necessary to ensure that each batch of a product is of the required quality and safety.

Personnel
- Personnel are required to have the appropriate qualifications, experience and training, and observe appropriate standards of hygiene.

Premises and equipment

- The design, location and construction of premises and equipment must be appropriate for the products being manufactured.

Documentation

- Documentation must permit tracing of batch history.

Production

- Production controls must ensure that products of the requisite quality are manufactured.

Quality control

- The system of quality control must ensure that all batches of products are in compliance with established specifications before their release.

Compliance with the *Australian Code of GMP for Medicinal Products* is ascertained by carrying out pre-licensing audits and, thereafter, regular on-site audits of manufacturers of medicinal products. The purpose of the audit is to assess compliance with the relevant manufacturing standard, the conditions specified in the manufacturing licence and with the relevant marketing authorisations relating to the medicinal products being manufactured. The scheduling and frequency of these audits is based on a risk-management approach that takes account of factors such as:

- type of product manufactured;
- the results of previous GMP audits;
- significant changes within the company, e.g., changes to key personnel, building, equipment or products;
- reports of adverse drug reactions and medicine problems;
- results of testing by TGA Laboratories arising from random or targeted sampling of products;
- recalls of products not meeting safety and/or quality standards;
- adverse comments from other agencies/bodies;
- post-licensing surveillance investigations; and
- intelligence "tip offs".

Most manufacturers are audited at two-yearly intervals, which is consistent with international practice. More frequent audits may be scheduled depending on the various risk factors outlined above. The TGA has GMP inspection agreements with other countries and organisations to obtain inspection reports, GMP certificates and other

GMP related information about overseas manufacturers exporting or wishing to export medicinal products to Australia.

4.3   POST-MARKET REGULATORY ACTIVITY

The streamlined approach to assessment for low-risk comple-mentary medicine products (Listed medicines) addresses the need to improve market access to quality, new complementary medicines, while maintaining public health and safety. It allows for timely mar-ket access, but with a level of pre-market evaluation of the compo-nents of each medicine that provides an assurance of the safety and quality of the product. However, to ensure a high level of public health and safety, an important feature of the TGA's risk manage-ment approach to both Listed and Registered complementary medi-cines is an appropriate level of post-market regulatory activity.

The essential elements of this systematic risk-based approach in-clude:

- targeted and random desk-based audits of Listed products;
- monitoring of adverse reactions to complementary medi-cines;
- targeted and random laboratory testing of products and in-gredients;
- targeted and random surveillance in the market place;
- an effective, responsive and timely recalls procedure
- audit of GMP; and
- effective controls for the advertising of therapeutic goods.

Laboratory Testing

Laboratory testing involves selecting random and targeted prod-ucts for analysis. As laboratory testing is resource and time-intensive, a risk-based approach guides all aspects of the testing program. The random testing of complementary medicines is linked to the random sample of products that are selected as part of the OCM's desk-based audit of Listed medicines for compliance with legislation. In addi-tion, testing occurs in response to problems identified by the OCM, Surveillance, Manufacturer Assessment, and Adverse Drug Reaction areas of TGA, by reports from overseas regulatory authorities and other areas.

Recall of Medicines

A procedure for the timely recall of medicines is an important post-market activity to protect public health and safety. Recalls are managed under the Uniform Recall Procedure for Therapeutic Goods 2001. This procedure is the result of an agreement between the therapeutic goods industry and Australian Government, State and Territory health authorities. It's purpose is to define the action to be taken by health authorities and sponsors when therapeutic goods for use in humans are to be removed from supply or use, or subject to corrective action, for reasons relating to their quality, safety or efficacy.

Overall responsibility for coordination of recalls lies with the Australian Recall Co-ordinator, who is an officer of the TGA. When the need for a recall has been established, the sponsor of the affected goods assumes the responsibility for recovery of the goods, or for corrective action, while the Australian Recall Coordinator assists by advising the sponsor of the procedures, by notifying agreed third parties and by monitoring the overall action. The objective of the TGA's post-market regulatory activities for complementary medicines is to support the timely identification and appropriate regulatory responses to problems with the formulation, manufacture, labelling and advertising of these medicines.

Complementary Medicines
which Do Not Need to Be Included in ARTG

Certain complementary medicines are exempt from Listing or Registration by the TGA. These include:
- raw herbs (unless packaged for supply as a therapeutic good);
- starting materials (unless packaged for supply as a therapeutic good or formulated as a dosage form);
- homoeopathic medicines (conditions apply);
- personal use imports (conditions apply);
- medicines used solely for experimental purposes in humans (conditions apply); and
- medicines dispensed or extemporaneously compounded for a particular person for therapeutic application to that person (this allows complementary healthcare practitioners, such as herbalists and homoeopaths, to prepare medicines for individual patients). Access to some medicinal ingredients is restricted by State and Territory legislation.

4.4   Adverse Reactions

A key focus of The National Strategy for Quality Use of Medicines (QUM) is to ensure that all medicines are used safely - minimising misuse, overuse and under-use of medicines and taking appropriate actions to solve medication problems such as adverse events, including interactions between complementary medicines and other medicines.

Adverse Drug Reaction Reporting System

An adverse reaction reporting system for therapeutic goods in Australia is well established. The Australian "Blue Card" system is a voluntary reporting system that covers all medicines and most health professionals. In addition, sponsors of all medicines included in the Australian Register of Therapeutic Goods (ARTG) are under an obligation to report adverse reactions to the TGA. The TGA's Adverse Drug Reactions Unit (ADRU) considers that some sponsors of complementary medicines have not been aware of their reporting obligations.

Recent amendments to the *Therapeutic Goods Act 1989* have imposed additional reporting requirements on sponsors and manufacturers to help ensure that they notify the TGA about adverse events in connection with the use of therapeutic goods. While a very high proportion of reports to the TGA from sponsors about conventional medicines originate from health professionals, the majority of reports from sponsors about complementary medicines appear to originate from consumers. Adverse reaction reports received by the TGA for both Registered and Listed medicines are entered into the Adverse Drug Reaction (Reporting) System (ADRS) database.

Reports of serious reactions are initially reviewed by a medical officer in ADRU and, additionally, are reviewed by the Adverse Drug Reactions Advisory Committee (ADRAC), which meets eight times a year. In addition, ADRAC reviews all reports of reactions (whether serious or not) to complementary medicines, vaccines, and new drugs (those marketed in the last three years). A summary of all reports to complementary medicines, including ADRAC/ADRU comments, is sent to the Complementary Medicines Evaluation Committee (CMEC) for comment and advice to the TGA.

Laboratory testing of medicines or enforcement activity (via the TGA's Surveillance Unit) may be arranged by ADRU in consultation with the TGA's Office of Complementary Medicines (OCM) before a report is reviewed by ADRAC, or on the advice of ADRAC, or on the advice of CMEC. ADRU performs literature searches and obtains advice from the OCM relating to the safety of complementary medicines.

The Australian Adverse Drug Reactions Bulletin, a quarterly publication, provides useful information on adverse reactions, including important issues arising from reports submitted to ADRAC. The Bulletin is distributed to medical practitioners, pharmacists and other health professionals and is available electronically at: *http://www.tga. gov.au/adr/aadrb.htm* .

International Collaboration on ARDS

As well as receiving Australian reports of adverse reactions, the ADRU has regular meetings with overseas agencies. In 1968, the World Health Organization (WHO) instigated a system of international collaboration in the monitoring of adverse drug reactions (ADRs). The aim was to make it easier to detect adverse drug reactions not revealed during clinical trials, with the aid of combined reports from a number of countries.

Some years later, the WHO Collaborating Centre for International Drug Monitoring was created in Uppsala, Sweden (the Uppsala Monitoring Centre; UMC). National drug-monitoring centres in around 54 countries currently interchange adverse reactions information via the UMC. ADRU is a member of the WHO pharmacovigilance network, and has access to the WHO international database of adverse drug reaction reports.

Recent Improvements to the TGA's Adverse Drug Reaction Reporting System for Complementary Medicines

The TGA has recently updated the existing framework of reporting and assessing suspected adverse reactions to medicines and that this could provide a useful starting point for developing a systematic complementary medicines adverse reaction reporting system. Recent improvements to support greater reporting of adverse reactions to complementary medicines include:
- ADR reporting may now be made via a web interface. It is thought that this may increase ADR reporting from those groups who do not generally report via the Blue Card system, which includes both consumers and complementary medicine practitioners;
- a "1-800" telephone number has been established to facilitate

reporting of adverse reactions (telephone 1800 044 114);

- an advertisement entitled "Adverse Drug Reactions Reporting Online" was placed in the Journal of the Australian Traditional-Medicine Society, 9(2), 101 (2003), promoting the web-based reporting system; and
- the ADRS has been upgraded. While this has not improved "searchability" in relation to complementary medicines (that is, most complementary medicines are still entered into the database by product name rather than by active ingredients), the TGA's new Strategic Information Management Environment (SIME) makes it much easier to determine the ingredients of a product on the ARTG, which facilitates the TGA's task of analysing complementary medicine reports.

The TGA has a continuous program of developing and improving its computer software. The ability to search for a single active ingredient across multiple products in the ADRS database would be an extremely useful addition.

Adverse Reaction Reports in Australia

In 2002, approximately 94 per cent of ADR reports received by the ADRU related to prescription medicines, and 3 per cent each to over-the-counter (OTC) and complementary medicines. The small number of reports received by the ADRU of suspected adverse reactions to complementary medicines is considered to be, in part, due to the fact that complementary medicines are, by and large, low risk products and have a low propensity for adverse effects. It is also due, in part, to the fact that the current ADRAC system is potentially biassed away from complementary medicines because complementary medicines are usually self-prescribed and their use may not be reported should a problem arise.

Among the factors that may contribute to under-reporting is that consumers may presume that complementary medicines are safe, use them without the supervision of a healthcare practitioner, and may be unaware of who regulates them. The TGA has indicated that, with some adjustments, the existing ADRAC framework of reporting and assessing suspected adverse reactions to medicines could provide a useful starting point for developing a systematic complementary medicines adverse reaction reporting system. In 2001, ADRU received 11,118 reports of suspected adverse reactions to medicines in Australia.

5.0 AUSTRALIAN REGULATORY GUIDELINES FOR COMPLEMENTARY MEDICINES

The TGA, in consultation with the Australian Self-Medication Industry (ASMI) and the Complementary Healthcare Council of Australia (CHC), is developing regulatory guidelines specifically for complementary medicines. A Consultation Group, comprising members from the TGA, ASMI and CHC with experience in the regulation and manufacture of complementary medicines, was established to assist in the development of a draft of the Australian Regulatory Guidelines for Complementary Medicines (ARGCM) for stakeholder consultation. This document is found at *www.tga.gov.au/docs/html/argcm.htm* . As development of the new complementary medicine guidelines has proceeded, the draft documents have been published on the TGA's website to allow comment.

The content of the ARGCM is intended to reflect both the nature of complementary medicines and the current Australian requirements for their regulation. The ARGCM will:

- provide information to help sponsors of complementary medicines to meet their obligations under therapeutic goods legislation;
- help ensure that applications to the TGA relating to complementary medicines uniformly meet all essential regulatory requirements so that applications may be processed successfully within minimum time frames; and
- enhance clarity and transparency of processes leading to the Registration and Listing of complementary medicines in the ARTG.

6.0 NEW LEGISLATIVE PROVISIONS AND OFFENCES TO STRENGTHEN THE NATIONAL REGULATORY FRAMEWORK

The Government introduced legislation to strengthen the regulatory framework to provide the TGA with enhanced powers to deal with breaches of regulatory requirements, and to address difficulties that have arisen as a result of the Pan Pharmaceuticals Limited recall. The legislative amendments were passed by the Australian Parliament and received Royal assent on May 27, 2003.

The purpose of the amendments was to tighten the existing requirements placed on manufacturers and sponsors of therapeutic goods, to further ensure the quality, safety and efficacy of therapeutic goods that are supplied in, or exported from, Australia. The need for these amendments was identified after the failure of Pan Pharmaceuticals Limited to meet the requirements of good manufacturing practice, and the difficulties encountered in quickly identifying affected therapeutic goods for the purposes of recall.

The experience highlighted the need to more clearly define the responsibilities and obligations of both sponsors and manufacturers of therapeutic goods, and the need for such persons to be held more accountable for their statutory responsibilities and obligations. The offences and penalties were considered to require strengthening, to provide a more adequate deterrent to breaches of standards and other statutory requirements designed to maintain the safety and quality of therapeutic goods. The increased penalty levels are higher than for similar offences in the Criminal Code, such as falsifying documents, because of the potential to expose the general public to an unacceptable level of risk.

A summary of the legislative amendments is given below:

- increase in the maximum penalties for a range of existing offences under the Act, including where there has been a failure to comply with standards, false statements made in applications for entry of goods on the ARTG, breach of a condition of a manufacturing licence (including failure to comply with the manufacturing principles), false statements made in a conformity assessment declaration and the counterfeiting of therapeutic goods;
- new penalties for falsification of any document that has been created, retained or issued for the purposes of the Act, and for supplying goods originating from a manufacturer or manufacturing site that has not been notified to the Secretary;
- expansion of the compulsory public notification and recall provisions which may be used where there is a problem with a product or its manufacture
- insertion of a "fit and proper person" test into the provisions for granting a manufacturing licence or conformity assessment certificate and suspending or revoking a manufacturing licence or conformity assessment certificate;
- insertion of new statutory conditions of licence to ensure compliance with the manufacturing principles and reporting of adverse effects known to a manufacturer;
- requirement for sponsors of therapeutic goods to maintain records of all manufacturers involved in the manufacture of each batch of therapeutic goods, and have them available for

inspection at any time, or risk cancellation of the goods from the ARTG, as well as requiring them to notify the Secretary of any change of manufacturer;

- provision for better identification of therapeutic goods in the event of a recall or where a sponsor applies for re-entry to the ARTG of previously cancelled goods;
- requirement for inclusion of manufacturer details on the labels of medicines; and
- improvements for adverse event reporting for Listed goods.

7.0   FORTIFIED FOODS

The role of Food Standards Australia New Zealand (FSANZ) is to protect the health and safety of people in Australia and New Zealand through the maintenance of a safe food supply. FSANZ is a partnership between ten governments: Australia, Australian States and Territories; and New Zealand. It is a statutory authority under Australian law and is an independent, expert body. It is responsible for developing, varying and reviewing standards and for developing codes of conduct with industry for food available in Australia and New Zealand covering labelling, composition and contaminants. In Australia FSANZ also develops food standards for food safety. The web site for FSANZ is *www.foodstandards.gov.au* .

The FSANZ Board approves new standards or variations to food standards in accordance with policy guidelines set by the Australia New Zealand Food Regulation Ministerial Council.

Vitamins or minerals are not permitted to be added to general purpose foods unless the addition of that vitamin or mineral is specifically permitted in *Standard 1.3.2-Vitamins and Minerals* and the vitamin or mineral is in a permitted form as specified in the Schedule to Standard 1.1.1 of the Code.

8.0   AUSTRALIAN AND NEW ZEALAND THERAPEUTIC PRODUCTS REGULATORY AGREEMENT

On December 10, 2003, the Australian and New Zealand governments signed an agreement to establish a joint regulatory scheme for therapeutic products. This joint agreement will regulate medicines, including complementary medicines, and medical devices and is expected to come into force in July 2005, subject to the passage of legislation and ratification of the treaty. A project team of Australian and New Zealand officials will work together to develop the final details of the new regulatory framework and the legislation to regulate therapeutic products in these two countries. The Trans-Tasman Therapeutic Products Agency Project is the name of this joint scheme. The web site containing all the details of the agreement is located at: *www.jtaproject.com/* .

In summary this scheme will cover:

- regulation of the manufacture, supply, import, export and promotion of therapeutic products;
- setting of standards in relation to the quality, safety, and efficacy or performance of therapeutic products and their manufacture, supply, import, export and promotion;
- post-market monitoring of therapeutic products; and
- enforcement of the requirements of the joint scheme.

The key elements of the regulatory framework for therapeutic products are:

- pre-market assessment of product safety, quality and efficacy;
- licensing of manufacturers to assure product quality; and
- post-market monitoring of product safety and quality, and surveillance to check for compliance.

There is a tiered structure to the legal instruments that comprise the new joint scheme for Australia and New Zealand:

- The Agreement is a "high level" agreement (or treaty) between the two countries;
- The implementing legislation will give effect to the Agreement and also contain those provisions that warrant being in legislation (e.g., fundamental accountability mechanisms and criminal offences); and
- Much of the detail to make the Agreement work will be contained in the Rules (made by the Ministerial Council) and Orders (made by the Managing Director).

Appendix 3

Canada

1.0   Definition of a Natural Health Product

The definition of a natural health product has two components: function and substance.

The function component refers to the natural health product definition capturing those substances that are manufactured, sold or represented for use in:

- the diagnosis, treatment, mitigation or prevention of a disease, disorder or abnormal physical state or its symptoms in humans;
- restoring or correcting organic functions in humans; or
- modifying organic functions in humans, such as modifying those functions in a manner that maintains or promotes health.

The substance component refers to the medicinal ingredient in a natural health product. These substances include, but are not limited to, traditional herbal remedies, traditional Chinese herbal remedies, Ayurvedic and Native North America medicines, homeopathic medicines, vitamins and mineral supplements, probiotics, amino acids and essential fatty acids.

The formal definition of included NHP substances is found in Schedule 1 of the NHP Regulations and this is:

1. A plant or a plant material, an alga, a bacterium, a fungus or a non-human animal matter.
2. An extract or isolate of a substance described in item 1, the primary molecular structure of which it had prior to its extraction of isolation.
3. Any of the following vitamins; biotin, folate, niacin, pantothenic acid, riboflavin, thiamine, vitamin A, vitamin B_6, vitamin B_{12}, vitamin C, vitamin D, vitamin E.
4. An amino acid.
5. An essential fatty acid.
6. A synthetic duplicate described in any of items 2 to 5.
7. A mineral.
8. A probiotic.

The Natural Health Products Directorate, Health Canada web site is at: *http://www.hc-sc.gc.ca/hpfb-dgpsa/nhpd-dpsn/index.html* .

2.0   PRODUCT LICENSING

Part 1 of the *Natural Health Products Regulations* sets out requirements for product licensing and the responsibilities of the product licence holder. The Regulations require an individual to obtain a product licence prior to selling an NHP in Canada.

The following guidance documents set out more information:
• Product Licensing Guidance Document;
• Evidence for Quality of Finished Natural Health Products;
• Evidence for Safety and Efficacy of Finished Natural Health Products;
• List of Acceptable Non-medicinal Ingredients;
• Compendium of Monographs;
• Homeopathics Guidance Document; and
• The Adverse Reaction Reporting Guidance Document-For Health Care Providers and Consumers.

2.1   STANDARDS OF EVIDENCE

Products are divided into two categories according to the claim:
• traditional use claims; and
• non-traditional use claims.

Types of claims are the following:

1. Treatment claims relate to the diagnosis, treatment and mitigation or prevention of a disease, disorder, or abnormal physical state or its symptoms in humans.
2. Risk reduction claims describe the relationship between using a medicinal ingredient and reducing risk of developing a specific disease or abnormal physiological state, by significantly altering a major risk factor or factors recognized to be involved in the development of the chronic disease or abnormal physiological state.
3. Structure function claims describe the effect of a medicinal ingredient on a structure or physiological function in the human body, or a medicinal ingredient's support of an anatomical, physiological, or mental function.

In general, the types of evidence to support the claims and their conditions of use can be categorized into the following categories:
- references to traditional use;
- references to scientific evidence;
- references from Expert Opinion Reports;
- references from reputable regulatory authority reports; and
- references to previous marketing experience.

The applicant may use any of the previous types of evidence as long as the evidence meets the requirements of the category of the claim (i.e., for a traditional use claim the applicant must submit two independent references that support the traditional use and the conditions of use) and is sufficient to support the type of claim being made. The guidance documents listed in Product Licensing (2.0, above) are applicable to this area of Standards of Evidence and more specifically, the Evidence for Quality of Finished Natural Health Products and Evidence for Safety and Efficacy of Finished Natural Health Products guidance documents.

3.0   SITE LICENSING

Part 2 of the Natural Health Product Regulations (Site Licences) sets out the requirements for site licensing and the responsibilities of a site licence holder. A site licence, in accordance with the Good Manufacturing Practises (GMP's), is required for manufacturers, packagers, labellers and importers of natural health products. The product licence application must also include the Site Licence numbers for all manufacturers, packagers, and labellers of the natural health product. If the natural health product is imported, the product licence application must include similar information with respect to all foreign sites performing any regulated activities. A Site Licence Guidance Document was prepared and is available on the NHPD website.

4.0   GOOD MANUFACTURING PRACTISES

Part 3 (Good Manufacturing Practices) of the *Natural Health Product Regulations* sets out good manufacturing practices - measures designed to ensure an effective overall approach to product quality control and risk management. They do so by setting appropriate standards and practices for product testing, manufacturing, storage, handling and distribution. The Good Manufacturing Practices Guidance Document outlines the requirements in detail for the manufacturing, packaging, labelling, importing and distributing of natural health products.

The Good Manufacturing Practices Guidance Document was prepared and is available on the NHPD website.

5.0   ADVERSE REACTION REPORTING

Within Part 1 (Product Licensing) of the *Natural Health Product Regulations,* Section 24 sets out the regulations for reaction reporting. A licensee has to produce a case report for each serious adverse reaction to the natural health product that occurs inside Canada, within 15 days of becoming aware of it. A licensee has to produce a case report for each serious unexpected adverse reaction to the natural health product that occurs inside or outside of Canada, within 15 days of becoming aware of it. A licensee who sells a natural health product shall annually prepare a summary report that contains a concise and critical analysis of (a) all adverse reactions to the natural health product that have occurred inside Canada and (b) all reactions for which a case report is required to be provided under the regulations, that have occurred during the past 12 months and at a dose used or tested for the diagnosis, treatment or prevention of a disease or for modifying organic functions in humans. Further if the Minister considers that a natural health product is no longer safe to be used under the recommended conditions, then further information can be required of the licensee. The Adverse Reaction Reporting Guidance Document-For Health Care Providers and Consumers was developed and is available on the NHPD website.

6.0 Fortified Foods and their Regulation in Canada

As the Canadian Parliamentary Bill C-420 was in second read-ing in March 2005 and as this Bill will move the *Natural Health Prod-ucts Regulations* which is currently a subset of the drug regulations to being a subset of the food regulations for the Canadian *Food and Drugs Act*, it was thought useful to briefly discuss the area of fortified foods.

Fortification is the addition of essential nutrients, especially vi-tamins and minerals, at levels above those normally found in the particular type of food to which they have been added, to address a deficiency or inadequate intake of the nutrient in the diet of people. Vitamins and minerals may also be added to restore those lost due to food processing, to make a substitute food nutritionally equivalent to the food for which it is substituting, or to make a special purpose food, including sole sources of nutrition.

In Canada the legislation for the addition of vitamins and miner-als to ordinary foods is of the "General Permission" type. General Permission refers to the situation where nutrient addition is regu-lated by legislation which specifies the foods and /or nutrients per-mitted and also the levels of the nutrients which might be permitted. In Canada's case, the allowed nutrients and their levels are specified in foods.

The addition of vitamins and minerals (micronutrients) to foods in Canada is controlled under regulatory provisions first promulgat-ed in 1964 (*Part D, Division 3, Food and Drugs Regulations*). *The Food and Drug Regulations* specify the foods to which micronutrients may be added, the micronutrients and the levels to which they may be added to these foods. The regulations state the amount of nutrient that must be present in the food at the time of purchase.

To add to the list of foods that may contain added micronutrients or to the list of nutrients, an amendment is required in the *Food and Drug Regulations*. The criteria for determining the acceptability of a nutrient addition to a food are based on the Guidelines for the Ad-dition of Nutrients to Foods (Trade Information Letter Number 351) and the General Principles for the Addition of Essential Nutrients to Foods established by the Codex Alimentarius Commission. Health Canada is currently preparing new regulations for fortified foods.

APPENDIX 4

CODEX ALIMENTARIUS COMMISSION

1.0   INTRODUCTION

Codex Alimentarius Commission (Codex) refers to a United Nations/World Health Organization subsidary of which Canada is a member. Codex is mandated to set international standards for trade in all types of food products. The purpose of Codex is "...to guide and promote the elaboration and establishment of definitions and requirements for foods, to assist in their harmonization and, in doing so, to facilitate international trade." Codex restrictions on health product supplements have been adopted in several countries such as Germany. The web site is at *www.codexalimentarius.net/*

2.0   CANADA

Health Canada has stated that as Codex applies to food products and Canada's Natural Health Products Regulations are distinct from food regulations, the limits for chemicals such as vitamins and minerals considered within Codex do not apply to Canadian natural health products. Further, the Canadian Natural Health Products Regulations were developed as a subset of drugs from the Canadian Food and Drugs Act and not as a subset of food.

Recently (March 2005) in the Canadian House of Parliament, a specific parliamentary bill C-420) was put forward that will direct the *Canadian Natural Health Products Regulations* to be placed as a subset of food for the *Canadian Food and Drugs Act*. This bill has not been passed to date but, as it was considered by the Canadian parliament, it seemed useful to briefly consider the more recent deliberations of Codex in regard to vitamins and minerals as they are covered by the *Canadian Natural Health Products Regulations*.

3.0 CODEX COMMITTEE ON NUTRITION AND FOODS FOR SPECIAL DIETARY USES

The Codex Committee on Nutrition and Foods for Special Dietary Uses met on November 4, 2003 and moved the Guideline for Vitamin and Mineral Supplements from step 3 to step 5 in Codex's eight-step international food standard-setting process. The committee reached consensus on using safety evaluations and the risk assessment method to determine upper limits for vitamins and minerals. Previously this upper limit figure for vitamins and minerals was based on a recommended daily allowance.

4.0 VITAMIN AND MINERAL SUPPLEMENTS: INTERNATIONAL REGULATORY CLASSIFICATIONS

Throughout the world, individual countries have national regulations that designate vitamin and mineral supplements in three different ways and these are as:
- Food
- Drugs
- Food at a lower level; drugs at a higher level

These same vitamin and mineral ingredients can be used in products for the following purposes:
- Diet supplementation
- Prevention
- Treatment

Appendix 5

European Union

1.0   Herbal Medicinal Products in Europe

Detailed information on this topic is to be found at: *http://www. bah-bonn.de/arzneimittel/pflanzlich/wisseuro_en.htm* . Herbal medicinal products have a long tradition, and their scientific estimation and public interest in them keeps increasing. The European market for herbal medicinal products is appraised at about 5.6 million US$ (ultimate consumer prices) by IMS International. Apart from a guideline on the quality of herbal medicinal products, there has not been any European regulation for the assessment of efficacy and safety of these products for a long time. The former Directive 75/319/EEC obliged the Member States of the European Union to check all products in the market within a period of 12 years. This Directive was implemented differently in the Member States so that there are different legal provisions, procedures and assessment criteria, such as the re-registration procedure in Germany or the "Avis aux fabricants" in France. In addition, there were different traditions in the Member States as regards herbal medicinal products.

The European Marketing Authorization System

In the course of a stronger harmonization of the European marketing authorisation system for medicinal products, a new two-stage system was established in the European regulatory framework in 1993, divided into a centralised and a decentralised procedure. A centralised marketing authorisation - obligatory for products derived from biotechnology and optional for technologically advanced products - provides the opportunity that a marketing authorization is granted for all Member States of the European Union at the same time. In contrast, the decentralised procedure is based on the principle of mutual recognition of national marketing authorisations. Since January 1998, extension of national applications to other Member States has required utilisation of the decentralised procedure, apart from few exceptions. This is outlined in Directive 2309/93.

The decentralised procedure is of great importance for many herbal medicinal products. The principle of this procedure is that a marketing authorization for a medicinal product is granted in one Member State and is subsequently recognized by other Member States in corresponding applications. Within a certain period of time after the application has been filed, the competent authority of the Member State concerned has to grant a marketing authorization on the basis of the first authorization, unless there are grounds for supposing that the authorisation of the medicinal product concerned may present a risk to public health with regard to the quality, safety or efficacy of the product. If these objections cannot be resolved, a binding decision is made by a central authority in an arbitration procedure according to which the marketing authorization is recognized or refused. Thus, in practice, arbitration might result in a loss of existing marketing authorisations ("negative rebound effect"). This is particularly true in cases when an inappropriate negative decision is made in an arbitration procedure due to different assessment criteria in the Member States. Thus, harmonized assessment criteria for herbal medicinal products to be applied by the different authorities could be a desirable long-term objective in Europe. Herbal medicinal products, which contain known ingredients in most cases, do generally not dispose of all studies and documents indispensable for innovative medicinal products, like toxicity studies. Since it seems principally appropriate to assess medicinal products with well-known ingredients, which might have been in the market for decades, according to their lower risk potential, the European Commission re-defined the term "well-established medicinal use" within an amendment to Directive 75/318/EEC (today: Annex of the codified Directive 2001/83/EC and 2003/63). Thus, epidemiological data and further published scientific literature are to be used in the context of a marketing authorization procedure for medicinal products with known ingredients.

The Herbal Medicinal Products Working Party (HMPWP) of the EMEA

At the beginning of 1997, the European Agency for the Evaluation of Medicinal Products (*EMEA*) established the Ad hoc Working Group "Herbal Medicinal Products," composed of representatives of national health authorities, the European Commission, the European Parliament and the European Pharmacopoeia. In 1999, this working group became a permanent working party of the EMEA. The objective target of the group is the development of assessment criteria for a sufficient proof of quality, efficacy and safety of herbal medicinal products. Quite a number of existing guidelines was revised with regard to their suitability for the evaluation of herbal medicinal products and was adapted to their specific requirements. The existing guideline "Quality of Herbal Remedies" (1989) was also revised and republished as the guideline on "Quality of Herbal Medicinal Products" according to the current nomenclature. Each guideline is submitted to the expert public for discussion; the comments received are discussed in detail before final publication.

The Directive on Traditional Herbal Medicinal Products

Within the conclusions of the AESGP study *"Herbal Medicinal Products in the European Union"* (see above), it was recommended that some clarification be incorporated into the existing EC legislation for those herbal medicinal products which are safe, of appropriate quality and whose indications are exclusively based on adequate proof of efficacy through documented traditional use. This recommendation is primarily based on the fact that there is quite a number of preparations in several Member States of the European Union with a long tradition and high safety but whose efficacy can only hardly be proven according to the current requirements to clinical or bibliographic evidence. Based on two drafts of the British Medicines Control Agency (MCA), the European Commission published the draft Directive "Traditional Herbal Medicinal Products" for discussion. The Commission's proposal, which was adopted on 17 January 2002 and will pass through the European legislative procedure, i.e., the consultations in the European Parliament and the Council of Ministers, is no longer a Directive of its own but integrated in Article 16 of the codified Directive 2001/83/EC according to this article. Its provisions are to be restricted to traditional herbal preparations which are to be included in a specific list to be set up in the near future. The list is to refer to certain indications and composed substances and is to take account of dosage levels and methods of administration. The inclusion into the list is conditional on the product having been used for at least 30 years within the European Union, or 15 years within the EU plus 15 years outside. Like for all medicinal products, the quality of traditional herbal medicinal products has to be documented according to the European legislative requirements.

The new regulations provide the establishment of a special committee which is to deal with the compilation of monographs, on one hand on the "well-established medicinal use" level (e.g., Core-SPCs on the basis of ESCOP monographs) and on the other hand for traditional preparations. This committee might evolve from the existing Herbal Medicinal Products Working Party (HMPWP) of the EMEA. However, it is indispensable in this context to clearly distinguish between the "well-established medicinal use" and the traditional herbal medicinal products. This is the only way to guarantee that well-documented herbal medicinal products in Germany, which received their marketing authorization on the basis of bibliographic data and monographs, maintain their high indication claim and are not mixed up with traditional herbal medicinal products which hold their low indication claim on the basis of tradition and long-term experience. Directive 2003/63 describes the structure and format of the documents to be supplied for assessment. The Directive specifically mentioned herbal medicine and homeopathic medicine. For both, a reduced document can be submitted for evaluation. No mention is made of Traditional Herbal Medicinal products, and they may need to be treated as Herbal products.

2.0 EUROPEAN COMMISSION DIRECTIVES

Regulation (EEC) No 2309/93
See: *http://biosafety.ihe.be/EMEA/2309_93en.pdf*
Authorization and supervision of medicinal products for human and veterinary use and establishing a European Agency for the Evaluation of Medicinal Products.

This provides a mechanism to also review medicinal products similar to the mechanism outlined for biotechnology products (87/22/EEC). This Directive allows the European Agency to evaluate the environmental risk of GMO based medicinal products.
Directive 2001/83/EC:
See: *http://www.opbw.org/nat_imp/leg_reg/uk/ec_dir_2001_83.pdf*

This Directive puts under one heading several previous Directives plus their amendments. It covers all the medicinal products that are not covered under EEC No 2309/93, which describes the centralized evaluation of medicinal products.

Directive 2001/83 is based on several Directives. For natural products it includes:

- 65/65/EEC - provisions related to medicinal products;
- 75/318-319/EEC; 1999/83 - protocols to test proprietary medicinal products;
- 92/25/EEC - distribution of medicinal products;
- 92/27/EEC - labelling and package leaflets for medicinal products for human use;
- 92/28/EEC - advertising for medicinal products; and
- 92/73/EEC - regulations regarding homeopathic medicine.

This was amended by Directive 2002/98/EC of the European Parliament and of the Council of 27 January 2003, setting standards of quality and safety for the collection, testing, processing, storage and distribution of human blood and blood components and amending Directive 2001/83/EC. This was amended by Commission Directive 2003/63/EC of 25 June 2003, amending Directive 2001/83/EC of the European Parliament and of the Council on the Community code relating to medicinal products for human use.

The Directive defines:

Medical product - Any substance or combination of substances which may be administered to human beings with a view of making a medical diagnosis or to restoring, correcting or modifying physiological functions in human beings.

Substance: Any matter of origin of:

- Human;
- Animal (including microorganisms, organs, secretions, parts, extractions);
- Vegetable (including microorganisms, plants, parts of plants, extracts, secretions);
- Chemical.

Homeopathic products: Any product made from products, substances and compositions called homeopathic stock according to homeopathic pharmacopoeias. The Directive does not deal with medical products specifically made for one patient by a pharmacy.

The Directive requires a market authorization for each member state based on application and documents (monograph) as outlined in Annex 1 and amendments (see above).

Homeopathic medicine needs to be registered authorized, but is covered by regulations in each member state (Article 39). Documents for each country are to be reviewed by competent experts or by a competent 3rd party in case of imported goods. Authorization is for 5 years renewable on application. The application is to be reviewed within 90 days. Authorization refused for: 1) a harmful product, 2) efficacy is lacking and 3) composition is not declared. An EC Agency will deal with common decisions in member states. This is not for homeopathic medicine, which are regulated by state (Article 16 (2)). Packaging and leaflets are described and regulated. Manufacturing must be authorized.

Products are classified as:

- prescription: renewable, non renewable, special, restricted
- non prescription.

Wholesaling is accomplished by distribution authorization. Advertising is regulated (article 86) and medication for certain diseases cannot be advertised. Reporting of suspected adverse reactions to the competent authorities is done by a responsible person for each market authorization.

Directive 2003/63/EC:

See: *http://www.vvkt.lt/t_aktai/tfiles/223.pdf*

This describes market authorization for products based on a dossier or Common Technical Document (CTD). This is for any product for human use. The CTD includes:

Module 1: Administrative

Module 2: Quality summary

Module 3: Chemical and biological characteristics

Module 4: Non Clinical reports, and

Module 5: Clinical reports.

This Directive is for all products including and specifically mentioned Herbals and Homeopathic medicines, and orphan medical products (traditional medicine). For Homeopathic medicine (page 85) it is required to: use Latin nomenclature, provide data on stock and general quality requirements and toxicology assays if the product or stock is a toxic product, provide stability tests and provide registration. For herbals the following requirements are set out: they require a monograph, nomenclature including Latin product name, Scientific name, percentage strength, extraction method, physical data, and data on supplier and contractor. In addition the following is required: history of development, manufacturing process, method of use and quality control data and analysis. For orphan medicine a case can be made for well-established medicinal use. These documents mentioned above amend the *Council Regulation EEC No 2309/93* and Directive 2001/83/EC.

Vitamins and Minerals in Foods 2003/0262 COD

See: *http://www.foodlaw.rdg.ac.uk/pdf/com2003_0671.pdf*
This proposal was developed out of concern that when both foods are fortified and vitamins and minerals are ingested through supplements, the public may be provided with harmful levels of vitamins and minerals. The proposed regulation outlines the vitamins and minerals as well as their form in foods. A specific committee, the standing committee of Food Chain and Animal Health (initiated by *Regulation 2002/178*) will then determine the safe levels of these vitamins and minerals allowed in food. The allowed quantities will be based on the other vitamins and minerals ingested as supplements. A Register will be set up to list the vitamins and minerals in certain foods.

Food supplements 2002/46 EC:
See: *http://europa.eu.int/eur-lex/pri/en/oj/dat/2002/l_183/l_18320020712 en00510057.pdf*
This Directive provides for the vitamins and minerals that are allowed in packaged sales. The strength will be assessed by a Committee (Committee on Food Chain and Animal Health) and will be based on the total daily intake from all sources and the total allowable limit for the compound.

APPENDIX 6

FRANCE

1.0   BACKGROUND

In France, medicinal products are legislated and regulated by the *Public Health Code (Code de la Santé Publique)* which regulates the production, sales and use of medicinal products. The code is enforced by the French Agency for the Safety of Medical Products. The Code covers all medicinal products including herbal and homeopathic products. As part of the European Community, France also has to abide to the various directives issued by the European Union whose objective is to harmonize the circulation of medicinal products among members of the Union.

2.0   FRENCH ORGANIZATIONS INVOLVED IN THE REGULATION OF HEALTH PRODUCTS

a) The French Agency for the Safety of Medical Products - L'Agence Française de Sécurité Sanitaire des Produits de Santé (AFSSAPS)

L'AFSSAPS is a publicly-owned establishment of France created in 1998. It has the essential role of guaranteeing the independence and the scientific rigour of the evaluation and controls relating to all health care and cosmetic products. L'AFSSAPS conducts inspections and provides authorizations for approved medical products. Specific areas of responsibility include drugs, laboratory reagents, medical devices, blood products, cosmetic products, and genetic and cellular therapy products. Website: *http://agmed.sante.gouv.fr* .

b) The French Food Safety Agency - L'Agence Française de Sécurité Sanitaire des Aliments (AFSSA)

This Agency comes under the under the supervision of the ministries for Health, Agriculture and Consumption. AFSSA was created in 1999 pursuant to the law of July 1, 1998 relating to the public health surveillance and with the monitoring of the products intended for humans. Its principal purpose is risk assessment; it assesses the health and nutritional risks in food for human and animal consumption in France. This Agency has no enforcement authority but provides research, opinions, advice and recommendations on the safety of food available for human consumption.

Website: *www.afssa.fr*

3.0   EUROPEAN UNION ORGANIZATIONS

The European Agency for the Evaluation of Medical Products (EMEA)

Council Regulation 2309/93 created the EMEA, setting out its core tasks. The Agency's Inspections Sector deals with a number of these tasks, specifically those concerned with the coordination of the verification of compliance with the principles of Good Manufacturing Practice (GMP), Good Clinical Practice (GCP) and Good Laboratory Practice (GLP) and with certain aspects of the supervision of authorized medicinal products in use in the European Community. The Sector is responsible for co-ordinating any GMP, GCP or GLP inspections requested by the CPMP or CVMP in connection with the assessment of marketing authorisation applications and/or the assessment of matters referred to these committees in accordance with Community legislation. These inspections may be necessary to verify specific aspects of the clinical or laboratory testing or manufacture and control of the product and/or to ensure compliance with GMP, GCP or GLP and quality assurance systems. The Sector organizes and chairs regular meetings of EU GCP and GMP inspectors where harmonisation of inspection related procedures and guidance documents are developed. In addition as part of the Agency's responsibility for the coordination of the supervision of authorized medicinal products under practical conditions of use, the Inspections Sector, in cooperation with the EDQM, operates a Sampling and Testing Programme. Communication and action by Member States in response to suspected quality defects relating to centrally authorized medicines are also coordinated by the Inspections Sector. Apart from inspection and supervision related activities, the Agency has been given responsibility for issuing certificates of medicinal products in accordance with WHO requirements which confirm the status of centrally authorized medicinal products and GMP compliance of the sites manufacturing the pharmaceutical forms. The Sector also coordinates activities in connection with the GMP annexes of the various Mutual Recognition Agreements (MRA) that have been negotiated between the European Community and non European countries and is responsible for the organisation of the activities within the GMP priority action area of the PERF programme. Last but not least, the Sector provides secretarial support to the joint CPMP/CVMP Quality Working Party. While most scientific activities of the Agency are divided between medicinal products for human and for veterinary use, the tasks of the Inspections Sector are typically common to both types of products. The Inspections Sector forms part of the Veterinary Medicines and Inspections Unit within the Agency.

Website: amea.eu.int/

4.0   PRODUCT CATEGORIES

a) Herbal Medicines

The Public Health Code does not provide any legal definition of herbal medicinal products and does not distinguish between medicinal products made from chemical substances and those made from plants or natural substances. Herbal medicinal products fall under the definition of *Article L 5111-1 of the Public Health Code* which considers as medicinal product any substance or combination of substances which may be administered to human beings or animals with a view to making a medical diagnosis or to restoring, correcting or modifying physiological functions in human beings. It is also the definition provided in Directive 2001/83/EC.

All herbal medicinal products listed in the European and in the French pharmacopoeias (with the exception of 34) are subject to the Code and can only be prepared, used or sold by pharmacists or qualified herbalists. Magisterial (prepared in pharmacy for an individual patient) or officinals (prepared in pharmacy according to the indications of the pharmacopoeia and to be distributed to all clients of this pharmacy) formulas can only be prepared by pharmacists. For magisterial formulas, a marketing authorization is not needed. Medicinal plants are defined in the French pharmacopoeia (Monograph "Plantes médicinales," March 1991) as plants that have at least one part with medicinal properties.

b) Vitamins and Minerals

Except in very few cases, the addition of vitamins and minerals to ordinary food is not allowed in France.

c) Food Supplements

There are no specific regulations for food supplements in France except that the European Directive 2002/46/EC, which lays down specific rules for vitamins and minerals used as ingredients of food supplements, applies to France.

d) Homeopathic Medicines

The French Public Health Code defines as a homeopathic drug any medication obtained from products, substances or composition called homeopathic starting substances and produced according to a homeopathic process described in the European pharmacopoeia, the French pharmacopoeia or, if not available, in the pharmacopoeias officially used in another member state of the European Union. Homeopathic medicines are uniquely recognized within European Union pharmaceutical legislation by Directive 2003/63/EC (amending earlier Directive 2001/83/EC) which acknowledges the particular nature of homeopathic medicines and gives them special status and requirements alongside the rest of the conventional pharmacy. The main difference in requirements is that for single homeopathic medicines for which no therapeutic claim is made, proof of efficacy is not required for them to be put on the market. Otherwise, homeopathic medicines are treated as other medicinal products. However, all homeopathic products must be registered with the AFSSAPS.

Only homeopathic medicinal products which satisfy all of the following conditions may be subject to a special, simplified registration procedure:

i) they are administered orally or externally,

ii) no specific therapeutic indication appears on the labelling of the medicinal product or in any information relating thereto,

iii) there is a sufficient degree of dilution to guarantee the safety of the medicinal product; in particular, the medicinal product may not contain either more than one part per 10 000 of the mother tincture or more than 1/100th of the smallest dose used in allopathy with regard to active substances whose presence in an allopathic medicinal product results in the obligation to submit a doctor's prescription. There are currently more than 3000 remedies listed in the homeopathic materia medica. This list is continually being added to as new medicines are "proved", i.e., tested, for their therapeutic potential on groups of healthy humans.

5.0 REGISTRATION AND MARKETING AUTHORIZATION

To be commercialized, any medication industrially manufactured must receive a market authorization (Autorisation de Mise sur le Marché (AMM)) delivered by European or national authorities. These authorities are the European Agency for the Evaluation of Medical Products (EMEA) or the French Agency for the Safety of Medical Products. Requests submitted by laboratories are assessed according to scientific criteria for quality, safety and efficacy. There are two processes available: the European process is used when the medication is intended to be marketed in all members of the European Community and the national process in cases where the medication is intended for the national market only.

All drugs industrially manufactured which have not received a marketing authorization from the European Union must receive such authorization from the French Agency for the Safety of Medical Products to be distributed in France. There are no registered combinations of herbals and homeopathics. The current legal framework for abridged procedures does not permit the registration of combinations of medicinal plants (either homeopathic or not), vitamins and oligo elements. Such combinations (some exist in the market, e.g., "aspirin, caffeine and meadowsweet") require a completely new registration. Customarily, Community legislation would apply but the current legal framework for abridged procedures in France does not permit the registration of such combinations.

The registration procedure for herbal medicinal products is, in principle, the same as that for other medicinal products. According to the Public Health Code, any medicinal product manufactured by a pharmaceutical company must be given a marketing authorisation before being marketed or distributed free of charge. The marketing authorisation is granted based on a dossier as described by the AFS-

SAPS and in articles R.5128-5136 of the Code. However, for herbal medicinal products of traditional use, the marketing authorisation application may be made on the basis of an abridged dossier without all or part of the pharmacological, toxicological and clinical studies. The burden of proving the quality, safety and efficacy of herbal medical products falls on the manufacturer.

6.0   GOOD MANUFACTURING PRACTICES

The preparation, importation and distribution of all medications must be done in conformity with good practices determined by the Minister of Health (*CHP L5121-5*). The good manufacturing practices established by the European Union govern all drugs in France, including herbal medicinal products. When a "magisterial preparation"is prescribed by a physician to be prepared in the pharmacy, the pharmacist is responsible for ensuring the raw material used is pharmaceutical grade. All Member States also apply the manufacturing requirements of Council Directive 75/319/EEC to herbal medicinal products. Starting materials of herbal medicinal products are in principle controlled in accordance with the European Pharmacopoeia in all Member States. Inspections for GMPs are carried out in practically all Member States.

7.0   ADVERSE REACTION REPORTING

The adverse reaction reporting systems of the Member States also monitor herbal medicinal products insofar as they are authorized medicinal products. The effectiveness of existing pharmacovigilance systems can be demonstrated by several withdrawals of marketing authorisations for herbal medicinal products due to safety concerns in connection with certain plants. Consumer reports could give an improved picture of the spectrum of adverse reactions to herbal medicinal products. The degree of acceptance of reports obtained from consumers in the national pharmacovigilance systems varies from one country to another. In France, the pharmacovigilance relies on manufacturers, health professionals and health institutions to report adverse reactions. The pharmacovigilance is ensured by the AFS-SAPS.

APPENDIX 7

GERMANY

1.0   BACKGROUND OF REGULATION

In contrast to other countries in Europe, herbal medicines have a special status in Germany, beginning with the Imperial Decree of 1901 that permitted the trade of many botanical drugs outside pharmacies. This was incorporated into Articles 29 - 31 of the First Medicines Act (AMG) of 1961. The legal basis for modern drug laws in Germany is based on European Community Directives 65/65/EEC issued in 1965, plus Directives 75/318/EEC and 75/319/EEC, issued in 1975. Under the terms of these Directives all member states of the European Community pledged to establish a formal review of all medicinal products on the market at that time and to assure that they met appropriate standards for quality and purity. Products were to be reviewed for safety and efficacy and re-registered by 1990 in Germany.

Consequently, on August 24, 1976, Germany passed the Second Medicines Act (Arzneimittelgesetz 1976, or AMG 76), which went into effect January 1, 1978, and required that the entire range of medicines in the pharmaceutical market (including conventional drugs, as well as medicinal plants and phytomedicines) be reviewed by scientific committees. AMG 76 includes special sections on phytomedicines: Article 22 Abs. 2 Nr.2, Section Article 25 Abs., Article 36, Article 44, and Article 45.

In 1978 the Minister of Health established a series of commissions to review various categories of drugs, including an expert committee for herbal drugs and preparations from medicinal plants, Commission E. These commissions were situated at the Bundesges-undheit-samt (BGA), the Federal Health Agency, charged with reviewing and approving the safety and efficacy of all drugs. In 1994 the BGA became the Bundesinstitut für Arzneimittel und Medizinprodukte (BfArM), the Federal Institute for Drugs and Medical Devices. Their website is: *www.bfarm.de/de/index.php.*

According to the AMG 76, for preparations that were already on the market at that time, a transition period of 12 years was allowed, following European guidelines. During this time, the products remained on the market, but evidence of quality, safety, and effectiveness still required validation. The regulations were designed so that the manufacturer had to provide proof of pharmaceutical quality for traditional herbal ingredients, whereas evaluations of safety and effectiveness were relegated to the monographs to be published by Commission E (Steinhoff, 1997b). However, all drugs that came into the market after the law went into effect (1978) had to be evaluated according to the procedures for new drug approvals. This applied to herbal and conventional drugs alike. The manufacturer must apply every five years for an extension of the drug registration. Proof of quality, safety, and effectiveness applied equally; however, for safety and effectiveness, reference to bibliographic evidence was allowed for herbal drugs. These commissions scientifically evaluated the following number of medicines: from 1978 until September 1994: 1,369 conventional drugs, 360 herbal drugs, and 187 veterinary drugs. By the end of 1995, the total number of herbs evaluated by Commission E was 360, whereas the number of herb parts reviewed as preparations was at least 391. This seeming discrepancy is because in some cases there is a monograph for each of several parts from the same plant (e.g., Senna fruit and Senna leaf; Hawthorn leaf with flower, Hawthorn fruit, leaf, or flower respectively). For more information, see *http://www.heilpflanzen-welt.de/monographien/texts/german_ commission_e_monographs_introduction.htm* .

2.0   CURRENT SITUATION

Two Acts regulate the Natural Health Products in Germany: The ArzneiMittleGezetz (AMG 1976) and the Food Act. The AMG describes that all substances used in humans and animals to treat, heal, prevent, diagnose or sooth and heal sickness, suffering and damage, are Medicines. These Medicines must be approved for sale and are, unless indicated otherwise dispensed through a pharmacy. The Medicines include: Chemicals, Plants and parts, animal parts and microorganisms. Each approval must be given by a Commission after study. The application must include a monograph. Medicine not dispensed through a pharmacy include those for non-medical purpose, healing waters and salts and salt tablets, ingredients for soap and external use, and disinfectants, and plant and plant products labelled with German names. Medicine requires a prescription unless it is provided otherwise. Homeopathic medicines are exempt from approval and must be listed in the Homeopathic Register. Medicine quality must be included in the Arznei Buch after being assessed by a Commission.

Vitamins are generally seen as a medicine but with some controversy. Germany allows some vitamins (specifically A and D) in food (LGM 1974) but generally excludes any not strictly mentioned additives from food. The jurisprudence of the European Union shows that Germany does not allow the entry of foods containing other vitamins than the ones listed in LGM 1974. This is being fought by other EU states. Also from the jurisprudence, it is shown that Germany generally uses RDA times three as a cut off above which vitamins are considered medicines and must adhere to AMG 1976. For further information, see:

http://bundesrecht.juris.de/bundesrecht/amg_1976/index.html .

The main Act and Regulations is the AMG 1976 with updates. This is called the Arznei Mittel Gezetz, or the Act describing Medications. This Act regulates the quality, the workings, the efficacy and level of harmlessness of medications.

A Medicine consists of materials or preparations of materials for the use in human and animal bodies, for healing, prevention, diagnosis, or to sooth/alleviate sickness, suffering physical damage or symptoms. All materials are included under the AMG 1976 Act, including those pre-packaged, but excluding food stuffs as outlined in the Food Law.

"Medicine" includes:
- Chemicals - natural chemicals, mixtures, and solutions;
- Plants, Plant parts - prepared or not prepared;
- Animal parts from humans or animals; and
- Micro-organisms and their derivatives.
- Concoctions made by a physician or other licensed person specifically prepared for one person or case are exempt from

this regulation.

The Ministry of Health is the Regulator and enforcer of the AMG 1976 Act. Medicines cannot be sold that are not prepared, that overstate quality, overstate safety and are of questionable quality. Permission for the manufacturing of medicine must be obtained from the Lander (provincial or State, not Federal) government. Qualifications for manufacturers are outlined. Medicine can be marketed only with an Approval from the Federal Government or from the EU Commission based on 2309/93. An Approval is not required for clinical testing. The Application process and content of documents for application are outlined. Approvals from other EU States can be used as documentation.

Specific commissions have been set-up to review Applications: Phytotherapy, Homeopathy, Anthroposophy (article 26(6)). Homeopathy preparations for all uses and in all packaging needs to be registered in the Register of Homeopathic Medicines where sales are > 1000 units/year. No approval is required to market Homeopathic Medicines that are Registered.

All Medicine is sold to the public through a pharmacy, except those for:

- non-medical purposes;
- waters, salts, and salt tablets;
- earth products for bathing, soaps for external use;
- plant, plant products and mixtures, pressed products, juices with German names on the label; and
- disinfecting products.

The above classifications also refer to products that are not on prescription, not harmful and not restricted otherwise. The retail sale of medicine not sold in a pharmacy is only allowed through knowledgeable persons. All Medicine under AMG 1976 Act is sold on prescription.

Medicine can be sold without prescription if the workings are known and the product does not need to be dispensed through a Pharmacy. If this requirement has ended after five years and is not renewed, the requirement is otherwise waived. The manufacturer must prepare a document providing the experience with the Medicine for review after being on the market for two years. This is a review of any adverse reactions for the product Manufacturer and wholesaler must ensure product quality. A specific person must be dedicated to monitor this. The quality must be described in the "Arznei Buch" and must include or adhere to the German rules and the EU rules set by the German and EU Commissions for Arznei Buch. (Pharmaco-poeia). Research and testing results are centrally collected and tabulated. Workings and drug interactions are documented and centrally collected and tabulated. All information is stored at the Deutsche Institut fur Medizinische Documentation. Risks of food additives are described in a paper by the Bundes Ministerium fur gezundheitlichen verbrasucherschutz und vertrinar Medicine (2002). This is to be found at: http://www.lebensmittelmeister.de/Informatives/BgVV/mineralstoffe.pdf.

This document describes the risk of oversupply of minerals from food when minerals are added to food. The report also describes a review of minerals in fortified products, and recommends the highest tolerated levels as to not surpass the UL (upper level) from all minerals from food and supplement intake. The following report concludes that the new EC regulations need to be more selective for considering tolerable and safe levels of minerals.

http://bundesrecht.juris.de/bundesrecht/lmg_1974/index.html

LMG 1974 - This law concerns the trade in food, tobacco products cosmetics and preservatives. This law describes what a food is: Materials in non-changed form, prepared or manufactured for human consumption, except those not for nutritive or pleasure use.

Additives: Materials defined as to affect the life or use of foods:
- minerals and micronutrients;
- amino acids;
- vitamin A and D;
- sweeteners; and
- other process additives.

Paragraph 15 states that it is not allowed to market animal-based products as food when they have pharmacological qualities. Paragraph 18 states that medical/pharmacological quality cannot be given to foods. Paragraph 33 states that all foods are described with "Guiding Principles" in the German Food Book, as assessed by the Food Book Commission (Lebensmittelbuch Kommission), based on testing and research and evaluation. For details, see:

http://europa.eu.int/comm/internal_market/en/goods/infr/469.htm

Germany - Barriers to the Import of Food Supplements

The Commission has decided to refer Germany to the Court on the question of barriers to the sale of vitamin-enriched food supplements imported from other Member States. Because of the levels of vitamins in these products, the German authorities classify some of them as medicinal products. The effect of this classification is that they are subject to a long and costly authorization procedure. However, the Commission considers that the systematic application of a purely quantitative criterion (three times the recommended daily intake) to classify a vitamin supplement as a medicinal product disregards the differences between the various types of vitamins and the different levels of risk involved in the event of excessive consumption. A less restrictive measure would be to specify a limit value for each vitamin, above which a preparation would be regarded as a medicinal product. The German authorities have so far refused to remove this obstacle.

Appendix 8

Hong Kong

1.0 Background

The policy for the future development of Chinese medicine was enshrined in the Basic Law of the Hong Kong Special Administrative Region. Article 138 of the Basic Law provides that "the Government of the Hong Kong Special Administrative Region shall, on its own, formulate policies to develop western and traditional Chinese medicine and to improve medical and health services. Community organizations and individuals may provide various medical and health services in accordance with law."

The Secretary for Health and Welfare conducted a public consultation on the development of Chinese medicine in the Hong Kong Special Administrative Region in November 1997 to solicit public opinions. Based on the Preparatory Committee's recommendations and public views collected in the consultation, the Chinese Medicine Bill was introduced into the Legislative Council in February 1999 and was passed in July 1999.

2.0 The Chinese Medicine Ordinance (1999)

Chinese medicines have been widely used in the community and play a very important role in the public health care services in Hong Kong. The *Chinese Medicine Ordinance* (Cap. 549) was passed by the

Legislative Council on 14 July 1999 to promote the development of Chinese medicines, and to strengthen the regulation on Chinese medicine. The regulatory system for Chinese medicine constituted under this ordinance is designed to safeguard public health, and at the same time, strengthen the position of Chinese medicine.

3.0 THE CHINESE MEDICINE COUNCIL OF HONG KONG (1999)

The Chinese Medicine Council of Hong Kong is a statutory body established on September 13, 1999 under the Chinese Medicine Ordinance. It is responsible for the formulation and implementation of the regulatory measures of Chinese medicine.

Their web site is: *www.cmchk.org.hk/pcm/eng/idx_news.htm* .

This statutory, regulatory body comprises practising Chinese medicine practitioners, members of the trade of Chinese medicines, academics, lay persons and government officials. The Council is responsible for implementing the regulatory measures for Chinese medicine. For regulation of Chinese medicine practitioners, the Council has started work on the registration of Chinese medicine practitioners under the transitional arrangements and is formulating detailed measures on the examination and discipline of Chinese medicine practitioners. For Chinese medicines, upon completion of relevant subsidiary legislation, the Council will implement the licensing system of Chinese medicines traders and the registration system of proprietary Chinese medicines by phases. The safety, efficacy and quality of proprietary Chinese medicines will be assessed before the products are allowed to be registered. The dispensation, storage and labelling of Chinese herbal medicines will also be regulated.

The Chinese Medicines Board was established under the Chinese Medicine Council of Hong Kong. The committees established under the Chinese Medicines Board include:

(i) The Chinese Medicines Committee - mainly responsible on matters related to registration of proprietary Chinese medicines (pCms) and for the regulation of Chinese herbal medicines;

(ii) The Chinese Medicines Traders Committee - mainly responsible on matters related to licensing of Chinese medicines traders; and

(iii) The Regulatory Committee of Chinese Medicines Traders - mainly responsible for the supervision and regulation of the professional practice and conduct of Chinese medicines traders.

The committees will make recommendations on relevant regulatory measures to the Chinese Medicines Board, and carry out any other functions assigned to them under the *Chinese Medicine Ordinance*, or as delegated by the Chinese Medicines Board. The Chinese Medicine Division of the Department of Health is responsible for providing administrative support and to implement the regulatory measures to, the Council, the Chinese Medicines Board and the committees.

According to the *Chinese Medicine Ordinance*, no person shall sell, import or possess any pCm in Hong Kong unless it is registered. Those who wish to register their pCms have to submit their application to the Chinese Medicines Board with all the required documents. After the assessment and approval by the Chinese Medicines Board, the pCm under application can then be registered. According to section 128 of the *Chinese Medicine Ordinance*, an applicant may apply for transitional registration for a pCm that was, on 1 March 1999, manufactured, sold or supplied for sale in Hong Kong.

4.0   REGULATION OF CHINESE MEDICINE (CM) PRACTITIONERS

CM practitioners are regulated through a system of examination, registration and discipline. In the long run, only registered CM practitioners are allowed to practice in Hong Kong. To become a registered CM practitioner, one must have completed a recognized undergraduate degree course in CM practice and pass the licensing examination conducted by the Council. They must also comply with the code of practice and meet the requirements on continuing education. The *Chinese Medicine Ordinance* provides for transitional arrangements for CM practitioners who were practicing CM in Hong Kong on or before 3 January 2000. They could apply to become listed CM practitioners. Effective 1 March 2002, any unqualified person (neither a registered nor listed CM practitioner) who practices CM in Hong Kong contravenes the *Chinese Medicine Ordinance*. In 2003, the Council conducted the Registration Assessment for listed CM practitioners and the first universal Licensing Examination. At present, there are over 4,700 registered CM practitioners and 3,200 listed CM practitioners in Hong Kong.

5.0 REGULATION OF CHINESE MEDICINES

Chinese medicines are regulated through a licensing system for traders and a registration system for proprietary Chinese medicines (pCm). Chinese herbal medicines are not registered.Wholesalers and retailers of Chinese herbal medicines listed in Schedule 1 and Schedule 2 of the *Chinese Medicine Ordinance* as well as wholesalers and manufacturers of pCm must obtain a licence for their business. The licensing requirements focus on personnel, facilities and hygienic conditions of premises. Proper packaging, labelling and keeping of sales records are also required to facilitate audit trail and recall in case of adverse reactions. To help the traders meet the future regulatory standards, the CM Council has prepared practicing guidelines for each type of these traders. In addition, guidelines on Good Manufacturing Practice and Good Clinical Practice have been drawn up. All pCm are required to be registered before they are allowed to be on sale or manufactured in Hong Kong. Having extensively consulted the trade, the Council set out the registration requirements for pCm based on the criteria of safety, quality and efficacy. The subsidiary legislation on Chinese medicines was passed by the Legislative Council in January 2003. Applications for licence of Chinese medicine traders and registration of proprietary Chinese medicines began in May and December 2003 respectively. So far, about 6,900 applications for trader licences have been received and they are now being processed. Like CM practitioners, transitional arrangements are provided for Chinese medicines traders who were in the business on 3 January 2000 and pCm which were manufactured or sold in Hong Kong on 1 March 1999. A transitional licence or transitional registration of pCm will be granted if an application was made during the specified period (5 May to 15 July 2003 for transitional licence for traders or 19 December 2003 to 30 June 2004 for transitional registration of pCm).

5.1 HONG KONG CHINESE MATERIA MEDICA STANDARDS (HKCMMS)

To safeguard public health, objective safety and quality regulatory standards of Chinese herbal medicines are required. The Department of Health is committed to developing regulatory standards for 60 commonly used herbs. To take the initiative forward, an HKCMMS office with experts recruited from the Mainland and an International Advisory Board comprising of renowned local, Mainland and overseas experts were established. A scientific committee has also been formed to provide technical advice and to monitor progress on the development of HKCMMS. Laboratory and research work is being conducted and validated in collaboration with local universities and research institutions from the Mainland and overseas. Preliminary results of the first eight herbs are now available for deliberation at the second International Advisory Board meeting scheduled in February 2004. The next stage of work involving 24 herbs will commence in early 2004. The development of HKCMMS, alongside the regulatory and other infra-structural developments, will support the modernization and globalization of Chinese medicines, paving way for Hong Kong to develop into an international centre for Chinese medicine.

5.2   REGULATION OF CHINESE HERBAL MEDICINE (HERBS)

Under the Chinese Medicine Ordinance (Cap. 549), Chinese herbal medicine means any of the substances specified in Schedule 1 or 2.

There are two schedules for Chinese herbs:
a) Schedule 1 has 31 potent herbs for prescription use only; and
b) Schedule 2 has 574 commonly used herbs (OTC).

The following regulatory areas are covered:
a) licensed traders, exercise import / export control;
b) "nominated persons" to supervise the business;
c) record keeping for audit and recall purposes; and
d) range of requirements including proper packaging, storage and labelling of name, source and batch number.

5.3   REGULATION OF PROPRIETARY CHINESE MEDICINES (pCMS)

Proprietary Chinese Medicines are defined as any proprietary product composed solely of the following as active ingredients; (i) any Chinese herbal medicine; or (ii) any materials of herbal, animal or mineral origin customarily used by the Chinese; or any medicines and materials referred to in (i) or (ii). They are formulated in a finished dose form and known or claimed to be used for the diagnosis, treatment, prevention or alleviation of any disease or any symptom of a disease in human beings, or for the regulation of the functional states of the human body.

The following regulatory areas for proprietary Chinese medi-

cines are covered:
a) registration of a product with pre-market approval covering safety, quality and efficacy;
b) the level of evidence to be based on the level of claims/risk;
c) compulsory post-marketing adverse reaction reporting;
d) licensing of importers/exporters, record keeping for audit and recall;
e) licensing of manufacturers and use of Good Manufacturing Practices;
f) for basic herbs and processed herbs, Good Agriculture Practices, Good Laboratory Practices and Standards for the herbs and processed herbs; and
g) one time transitional arrangement with minimum requirements (e.g., heavy metal, pesticide and microbial limits).

5.3.1 PROPRIETARY CHINESE MEDICINES TO BE REGISTERED

According to section 119 of the *Chinese Medicine Ordinance* (CMO), all proprietary Chinese medicines shall be registered in accordance with section 121 of the Ordinance. No person shall sell, import or possess any pCm unless it is registered. Based on the claims, ingredients and pharmacological effects, products containing Chinese herbs can be classified into three main categories, namely proprietary Chinese medicines, western medicines and foods.

5.3.2 FORMAL DEFINITION OF PROPRIETARY CHINESE MEDICINE

According to the CMO, "proprietary Chinese medicine (pCm)" means any proprietary product that is:
a) composed solely of the following as active ingredients: (i) any Chinese herbal medicines; or (ii) any materials of herbal, animal or mineral origin customarily used by the Chinese; or (iii) any medicines and materials referred to in subparagraphs (i) and (ii) respectively;
b) formulated in a finished dose form; and
c) known or claimed to be used for the diagnosis, treatment, prevention or alleviation of any disease or any symptom of a disease in human beings, or for the regulation of the functional states of the human body.

The substances as described in (a)(i) and (a)(ii) above are referred to as the "Chinese herbs" in the Application Handbook for the Registration of Proprietary Chinese Medicines.

Products containing both Chinese herbs and western medicines are regarded as western medicine products, and are registered and regulated under the Pharmacy and Poisons Ordinance (Cap. 138).

Products that contain Chinese herbs and meet all the following criteria can be regarded as food (e.g., ShanZhaBing/Haw flakes), and shall be regulated under the *Public Health and Municipal Services Ordinance* (Cap. 132):

a) products used in form or manner of normal foods (e.g., to be taken orally, and usually with no recommended dose regimens);
b) products that do not claim any curative or health care function; and
c) all the Chinese herbs used in the product can generally be considered as food.

5.3.3 PROPRIETARY CHINESE MEDICINES EXEMPTED FROM REGISTRATION

According to the CMO and *Chinese Medicines Regulations*, the following pCms may be exempted from registration:

a) a pCm of a reasonable quantity that is manufactured by a manufacturer, or imported by a wholesaler of pCm, for the purposes of providing samples and seeking registration; (Reference: section 119(3), CMO)
b) a pCm that is required for the purposes of education or scientific research. The Chinese Medicines Board may exempt, with or without conditions or restrictions, a person or institution concerned with education or scientific research from the requirements for registration for the pCms in question; (Reference: section 158(1), CMO)
c) a pCm that is imported by a wholesaler of pCms for the purpose of re-exporting by the same wholesale dealer; (Reference: section 158(5)(a), CMO)
d) a pCm that is imported by a holder of a valid certificate for clinical trial and medicinal test and is to be used for the purposes of the clinical trial or medicinal test to which the certificate relates; (Reference: section 158(5)(b), CMO)
e) a pCm that is compounded by or under the supervision of a registered Chinese medicine practitioner or a listed Chinese medicine practitioner at the premises where he practises if, and only if, such pCm is being used for the purpose of ad-

ministering or supplying to a patient under his direct care; (Reference: section 158(6)(a), CMO)

f) a pCm that is individually prepared or compounded for one patient (i) by a person nominated under section 114(2)(b)(i) or (ii) of CMO; or (ii) under the supervision of such person, at the premises in respect of which a retailer licence is in force and in accordance with a prescription given by a registered Chinese medicine practitioner or a listed Chinese medicine practitioner. (Reference: section 158(6)(b), CMO)

g) (i) a pCm that is manufactured in the premises in respect of which a manufacturer licence is in force and by or under the supervision of a responsible person in accordance with a prescription given by a registered Chinese medicine practitioner, or a listed Chinese medicine practitioner; and (ii) a pCm that is, in the case where the medicine is for internal application or both internal and external application, to be administered or supplied to the patient to whom the prescription is given and who is under the direct care of the Chinese medicine practitioner; or in the case where the medicine is for external application only, and is to be administered or supplied to a patient or patients under the direct care of the Chinese medicine practitioner (one patient for internal application, and several patients for external application); and (iii) The Chinese Medicines Board has received from the manufacturer, at least one working day before the day on which the manufacturing process of the medicine begins, a written notification including the particulars set out in section 37(2) of the Chinese Medicines Regulation and being accompanied by an undertaking referred to in section 37(3) of the Chinese Medicines Regulation (Reference: section 37(1), Chinese Medicines Regulation).

6.0   Current Ongoing Areas (2004-2007)

The following are important areas being worked on in the area of Traditional Chinese Medicine in Hong Kong:

a) the completion of the regulations and guidance documents;
b) developing regulatory standards on herbs; and
c) setting up the adverse reaction monitoring system for herbals.

Appendix 9

India

1.0 Background

In India, the manufacture, sale and distribution of medicinal products come under the *Drugs and Cosmetic Act 1940* and Rules thereunder. The Act was introduced in 1940 and the Rules pertaining to the Act in 1945. The Act and the Rules have been amended numerous times since then. The legislation is national but its enforcement comes under the responsibility of Indian States. There are 24 states in India. Each state has a Drug Control Department or Food and Drug Administration responsible for enforcing the *Drugs and Cosmetics Act and Rules*.

Central Authorities are responsible for approval of new drugs, and clinical trials in the country, laying down the standards for drugs, control over the quality of imported drugs, coordination of the activities of State Drug Control Organisations and providing expert advice with a view of bringing about the uniformity in the enforcement of the Drugs and Cosmetics Act. The Drug Controller General of India is responsible for approval of licences of specified categories of drugs such as blood and blood products. The main regulatory web site for the Central Drugs Standard Control Organization is: *http://cdsco.nic.in/* .

The following are the main activities of the Drug Control Department of the State of Delhi, which is probably representative of the other States:

a) inspection for grant/renewal of licences for the manufacture of allopathic drugs including whole human blood/blood components/Blood products, surgical dressings, diagnostic reagents/ kits, disposable syringes/needles/perfusion sets, repacking of drugs, homoeopathic medicines and cosmetics;

b) inspection for grant/renewal of licences for retail and wholesale of drugs including homoeopathic medicines. No licence for sale of Ayurvedic/Unan /siddha medicines and cosmetics is required;

c) collection of samples of drugs and cosmetics from mfg./sale premises for test/analysis to check their quality being manufactured and sold in Delhi;

d) inspections and raids with a view to detect offences under the Act specially movement and sale of spurious drugs/ cosmetics;

e) investigations of cases of contraventions under the Act;

f) inspections of the premises licensed for manufacture and sale of drugs, with a view to ensure that conditions of the licences are complied with; and

g) launching of prosecutions against persons / firms found contravening the provisions of the Act.

The Drug Control Department also enforces:

a) the *Drugs & Magic Remedies (Objectionable Advertisement) Act*, 1954. Under the Act, various advertisements published in newspapers, periodicals and journals are scrutinized for objectionable advertisements. Investigations are carried out in all such cases where contraventions are observed. Appropriate action is taken and prosecutions are launched under the Act against the persons found publishing objectionable advertisements; *and*

b) the *Drugs (Prices Control) Order 1995.* Under this Order, sales premises are checked to ensure that drugs are sold at a price not exceeding the maximum retail price plus local taxes payable extra. Those found violating the said Order are prosecuted under the Essential Commodities Act, 1955 read with the

Drugs (Prices Control) Order, 1995. *The Drugs and Cosmetics Act* does not formally define Allopathic medicines. However, if specifically defines Ayurvedic and Homeopathic medicines. Drugs other than Ayurvedic and Homeopathic medicines are commonly known as Allopathic or modern medicines.

2.0   HERBAL PRODUCTS

The Drugs and Cosmetics Act, 1940 (the "Drugs Act") and the Drugs and Cosmetics Rules, 1945 (the "Drugs Rules") prescribe the standards and quality, and regulate the import, manufacture, sale and distribution of all drugs, including Ayurvedic, drugs in India. Under the Act, an Ayurvedic drug "includes all medicines intended for internal or external use for or in the diagnosis, treatment, mitigation or prevention of disease or disorder in human beings or animals, and manufactured exclusively in accordance with the formulae described in the authoritative books of Ayurvedic, Siddha and Unani Tibb systems of medicine, specified in the First Schedule" of the Drugs Act (Section 3(a) of the Drugs Act). The Drugs Act prescribes a particular standard for manufacturing an Ayurvedic drug for sale or for distribution. The drug manufactured should comply with the standards for identity, purity and strength as laid down in the editions of Ayurvedic pharmacopoeia of India. (Section 33 EEB of the Drugs Act r/w Rule 168 of the Drugs Rules).

3.0   GOOD MANUFACTURING PRACTICES REGULATION (GMP)

Manufacturing of Allopathic, Ayurvedic, Siddha, Unani and Homoeopathic drugs are regulated in the *Drugs and Cosmetics Rules, 1945* under different schedules for GMP provisions:
1. Schedule M - Allopathic Drugs [Rules 71/71-A&76]
2. Schedule MI - Homoeopathic Drugs [Rule 85-E (2)]
3. Schedule T - Ayurvedic, Siddha and Unani Drugs [Rule 157].

4.0   FOOD SUPPLEMENTS

There is no "dietary supplement" concept -as the United States defines it- in regulation, marketing, the medical community or consumer understanding. A draft law reminiscent of the Dietary Supplement Health and Education Act (DSHEA) is in development in India to regulate manufacturing, importing and marketing of health foods/ dietary supplements and other nutraceuticals. Also, the country's Central Drug Control Department has put some structures in place for dietary supplements, but it is taking a long time for states to co-operate, and some states have rejected the structures when their own rules and regulations conflict. This means companies interested in marketing dietary supplement products must work within the current structure under which all products are registered as either food or pharmaceutical. Generally the manufacturer decides which route to take when registering a product. An obvious challenge is that some manufacturers register products as drugs and other companies register comparable products as foods, creating confusion among consumers. Industry members familiar with this environment advise registering supplements as foods, because the pharmaceutical process is more complicated and takes longer. However, in some states, such as Karela, supplements must be registered as pharmaceuticals.[1] Licences for manufacturing food supplements are usually issued under the Prevention of Food Adulteration Act.

5.0   HOMEOPATHICS

The *Drugs and Cosmetics Act* defines drugs broadly and inclusively to include even homeopathic medicines. Thus, all provisions of the Act are applicable to homeopathic medicines as well, which means that the provisions relating to standards of quality, misbranded, spurious or adulterated drugs are equally applicable to homeopathic medicines as well. In this section, we will discuss those provisions of the *Drugs and Cosmetics Rules, 1945* (called the Rules) that incorporate standards exclusively applicable to Homeopathic medicines. The definition of homeopathic drugs may be found in the Rules as including any drug which is recorded in homeopathic provings or therapeutic efficacy of which has been established through long clinical experience as recorded in authoritative homeopathic literature of India and abroad and which is prepared according to the techniques of homeopathic pharmacy and covers combination of ingredients of such homeopathic medicines but does not include a medicine which is administered by parenteral route. Manufacture of Homeopathic medicines as well as New Homeopathic Medicines is governed by part VIIA of the Rules which provides that no person may manufacture for sale or for distribution, any Homeopathic medicine or New Homeopathic Medicine without a licence granted by the Licensing Authority. The grant of a manufacturing licence is subject to the man-

---

[1]   This text was taken from *Entering India's Dietary Supplement Market* by Suzanne Shelton, www.naturalproductsinsider.com/articles/271infoc.html

ufacturer adhering to the provisions of Schedule M1 to the Rules, which lay down the requirements for factory premises for manufacture of Homeopathic preparations.

Some important provisions of the *Drugs and Cosmetic Act, 1940* and the Rules made thereunder are:

a) homoeopathic medicines are defined under Rule 2(dd) of *Drugs and Cosmetics Rules, 1945.*

b) standards of Homoeopathic medicines to be complied for manufacture, for sale, distribution or import are defined under Second Schedule of the *Drugs and Cosmetics Act* (item N.4a).

c) new Homoeopathic medicines are covered under Rule 30 aa.

d) minimum requirements for good manufacturing are included in Schedule C1.

e) ophthalmic preparations, standards and conditions for preparation thereof are covered under Schedule ff (Rule 126 a).

f) Homoeopathic Pharmacopoeia Laboratory, Ghaziabad is to function as Central Drugs Laboratory with respect to Homoeopathic drugs, under section 6 of the act under sub-rule 7 of rule 3-a.

g) anybody can get medicines tested under Section 26.

h) under Section 26-a, Central Government can cancel licence of manufacturing a drug, if therapeutic claims are not genuine.

i) procedures for labelling and packing of Homoeopathic medicines are covered under Rule 32 a, Rule 106 a and 106 b(Part ix-a).

j) rule 85 b covers manufacture of mother tinctures, potencies or potencies from back potencies. Application for which is made under form 24 c.

k) rule 85 c and 30 aa covers manufacture of new Homoeopathic drugs.

l) individual pharmacists (shop keepers) are allowed to manufacture of potencies only and, that only from back potencies, under Rule 85 d.

m) retail is covered under Rule 67 c. An application can be made under form 20 c. Single drugs.

n) though whole sale is covered under Rule 67 c, but application is made under form 20-d. Single drugs.

o) licensing authority for issue of licence for Homoeopathic medicines lies with the State Government as per Rule 67 a and 85 b.

6.0   Adverse Reaction Reporting

There is no developed system for monitoring adverse reactions in India. It was reported that a more effective pharmacovigilance system is being introduced.[2]

7.0   Note on Ayurvedic Medicine

Ayurved is a science and the way of life, upang (a part) of Atharaved, is the first authentic record of medical knowledge of vedic period, useful for the preservation of health, cure of disease and maintenance of life in state of happiness. Ayur Vigyan, much more than a mere system of medicine involves correlation between science, technology and modern medicine with ayurved. The knowledge of pharmacy, pharmacology, chemistry, biochemistry, phytochemistry, botany, pathology, geology etc. is useful in deciding the identity, purity, quality of drugs. Though the *Drugs Act* was enacted in 1940, Ayurvedic drugs were brought within the purview of the Act only in 1964. Patent and proprietary Ayurvedic medicines are also recognized in view of the definition inserted under section of the Act. During last thirty-four years many steps have been taken for standardisation of the Ayurvedic medicines:

- 1978 - Ayurvedic formulary published by the Government of India;
- 1976 - Pharmacopoeia standards for Ayurvedic formulations published by Central Council for research in India Medicine and Homeopathy; and
- 1986 - Ayurvedic Pharmacopoeia published by the Government of India.

---

[2]   The Times of India, April 7, 2004).

APPENDIX 10

PEOPLE'S REPUBLIC OF CHINA

Information on the regulatory aspects of health foods, medicinal products and foods are to be found on national web sites in the Chinese language. The summary documentation was translated into English. A few non-government web sites that translated the Chinese documentation into English were also used. The State Food and Drug Administration is China's main federal regulator for traditional Chinese herbals. Their web site is: *http://www.sda.gov.cn/webportal/portal.po* .

A.   LAWS AND REGULATIONS

In China, health foods and medicinal products are regulated under two basic laws, namely the Food Hygiene Law and the Drug Administration Act of the People's Republic of China (PRC).

1.0   FOOD HYGIENE LAW PEOPLE'S REPUBLIC OF CHINA

"Food" means any product or raw material provided for people to eat or drink, as well as any product that has been traditionally served as both food and medicament, with the exception of products used solely for medical purposes.

Note:

- In this area there is potential legislative space for our definition of "Natural Health products."

- Foods that can also serve as medicament come from the Food Cures (Yao Shan) system of Traditional Medicine.

(Law Promulgation Date: 1995-10-30; Effective Date: 1995-10-30)

Contents:

- Chapter I: General Provisions (Articles 1-5)
- Chapter II: Food Hygiene (Articles 6-10)
- Chapter III: Food Additives Hygiene (Article 11)
- Chapter IV: Food Containers, Packaging Materials, Food Utensils and Equipment, and Facilities Hygiene (Articles 12-13)
- Chapter V: The Formulation of Food Hygiene Standards and Policing Methods (Articles 14-16)
- Chapter VI: Food Hygiene Control (Articles 17-31)
- Chapter VII: Food Hygiene Supervision (Articles 32-38)
- Chapter VIII: Legal Liabilities (Articles 39-53)
- Chapter IX: Supplementary Provisions (Article 54-57).

2.0   DRUG ADMINISTRATION ACT
OF THE PEOPLE'S REPUBLIC OF CHINA

Drugs refer to articles that are used in the prevention, treatment and diagnosis of human diseases and intended for the regulation of the physiological functions of human beings, for which indications, usage and dosage are established. Drugs include Chinese crude drugs, prepared slices from Chinese crude drugs, traditional Chinese medicine preparations, chemical drug substances and their preparations, antibiotics, biochemical drugs, radioactive pharmaceuticals, serum, vaccines, blood products and diagnostic agents.

The most current English version of the Drug Administration Law of the PRC was found at: www.lehmanlaw.com/lib/library/Laws_regulations/pharma/drug_admlaw.htm; the most current Chinese version is at: *www.fdc-law.com.cn/laws/detail_262.html* .

Contents:

- Chapter I: General Provisions (Articles 1-6)
- Chapter II: Regulation of Drug Production Enterprises (Articles 7-13)
- Chapter III: Regulation of Drug Management Enterprises (Articles 14-21)
- Chapter IV: Regulation of Drug Prescriptions in Medical Institutions (Articles 22-28)
- Chapter V: Regulation of Pharmaceutical Drugs (Articles 29-51)

- Chapter VI: Regulation of Packaging of Pharmaceutical Drugs (Articles 52-54)
- Chapter VII: Regulation of Pricing and Advertising of Pharmaceutical Drugs (Articles 55-63)
- Chapter VIII: Drug Supervision (Articles 64-72)
- Chapter IX: Legal Liabilities (Article 73-101)
- Chapter X: Supplementary Provisions (Articles 102-106).

In addition, there are Regulations on the Enforcement of the Drug Administration Act, enforced by various provisional measures for the various administrative functions regarding drug manufacturing, drug registration, drug distribution and drug importation.

Regulations on the Enforcement of the Drug Administration Act include:

- Provisional Measures for the Administration and Supervision of Drug Manufacturing;
- Provisional Measures for the Administration of Drug Registration;
- Provisional Measures for the Administration of Drug Distribution; and
- Measures for the Administration of Drug Importation.

B.   CHINESE GOVERNMENT ORGANIZATIONS INVOLVED IN THE REGULATION OF HEALTH PRODUCTS

1.0   STATE FOOD AND DRUG ADMINISTRATION (SFDA)

The State Food and Drug Administration (SFDA) was founded on the basis of its former counterpart, the State Drug Administration (SDA), and got its current name on April 16, 2003. SFDA is responsible for protecting public health by assuming the safety, efficacy and security of drugs, biological products, medical devices, the food supply and cosmetics. As a direct part of the State Council, SFDA has regulatory and legal enforcement functions in the supervision of these fields. The SFDA works with the following five regulatory committees to achieve its mandate.

a) National Institute for the Control of Pharmaceutical and Biological Products (NICPBP)

The NCIPBP is the statutory and the highest technical arbitration institute for quality inspection of pharmaceutical and biological products:

URL: *www.nicpbp.org.cn* (Official Chinese Web site).

b) National Pharmacopoeia Committee

The National Pharmacopoeia Committee formulates national drug standards through its publication, Pharmacopoeia of the People's Republic of China, as one of the national drug standards. Article 23 of the Drug Administration Act of the People's Republic of China states: "Drugs must comply with the national drug standard, or with the drug standard of the province, autonomous region or municipality under the direct control of the Central Government. The Pharmacopoeia of the People's Republic of China and the drug standards promulgated by the department of the State Council administering health are the national drug standards. The Pharmacopoeia Committee of the department of the State Council administering health is the body responsible for handling the setting and revision of national drug standards."

c) Centre for Drug Evaluation

Article 24 of the Drug Administration Act of the PRS states: "The State Council department responsible for health administration and the departments of the provinces, autonomous regions and municipalities under the direct control of the Central Government administering health may establish a Drug Evaluation Committee to evaluate new drugs and re-evaluate drugs already being produced." According to a presentation given at the First Natural Health Product Research Conference (February 20-22, 2004 in Montreal, Quebec) entitled ATCM Administration and Trade Briefing in China" by Ms. Zhenhua Liu, Second Secretary of the Economic and Commercial Counsellor's Office of the Embassy of People's Republic of China, the Centre for Drug Evaluation is also the governmental body involved in drug registration.

d) Certification Committee for Drugs

The Certification Committee for Drugs oversees the certification of drug products according to the Good Laboratory Practice (GLP), the Good Clinical Practice (GCP), the Good Sales Practice (GSP), the Good Agriculture Practice (GAP) and the Good Utilities Practice (GUP).

155

e) Centre for Drug Reevaluation

The Centre for Drug Reevaluation is in charge of re-evaluating drugs already being produced, and maintains the Drug Catalogue.

URL: *www.sda.gov.cn* (Official Chinese Web site) or *www.chinafdc-law.cam/laws/* (English version).

2.0   MINISTRY OF COMMERCE (MOFCOM)

The new Ministry of Commerce (MOFCOM) commenced operating on March 25, 2003, and integrates domestic and foreign trade functions. MOFCOM has assumed responsibility of the former Ministry of Foreign Trade and Economic Cooperation (MOFTEC) and the State Development and Planning Commission's (SETC) functions relating to internal trade, foreign economic cooperation, and organization and implementation of plans for the import and export of major industrial products and raw and semi-finished materials. In addition, MOFCOM is responsible for the functions of the former State Development and Planning Commission (SDPC) with respect to implementation of state planning for the import and export of agricultural products. The MOFCOM has 25 departments and offices, which have responsibilities in the following principal areas:

1. Drafting of trading and economic cooperation policies and laws, integrating Chinese laws with provisions of international treaties and agreements.
2. Domestic Trade and Distribution
3. Market Operations
4. Commodities Import and Export
5. Technology and Trade
6. International Relations
7. International Economic and Trade Organizations
8. Anti-dumping, Anti-Subsidy and Safeguards
9. Foreign Direct Investment in China
10. Foreign Economic Cooperation and Overseas Investment
11. Foreign Aid
12. Hong Kong SAR, Macau SAR and Taiwan
13. Overseas-based Delegations and Local Commercial Trade Associations.

Note: Information taken from the China and Law Policy Newsflash, July 30, 2003 PDF document URL:

http://wwwomm.com/webdata/content/publications/clp030730.pdf

URL: *www.cintcm.ac.cn/gam/e_index6.html* (Official Chinese Web-

site) or
www.english1.mofcom.gov.cn/mission.shtml (English version).

3.0 CHINA CHAMBER OF COMMERCE OF MEDICINES AND HEALTH PRODUCTS IMPORTERS AND EXPORTERS (CCCMHPIE)

The China Chamber of Commerce of Medicines and Health Products Importers and Exporters (CCCMHPIE) was established in May 1989 in an effort to boost the sound development of foreign trade in medicinal products. As a social body formed along business lines and enjoying the status of a legal person, the Chamber is composed of economic entities registered in the People's Republic of China dealing in medicinal items as authorized by the departments under the state Council responsible for foreign economic relations and trade as well as organizations empowered by them. It is designated to coordinate import and export business in Chinese and Western medicines and provide service for its members' enterprises. It has over 1100 members throughout China. The Chamber abides by the state laws and administrative statutes, implements its policies and regulations governing foreign trade, accepts the guidance and supervision of the responsible departments under the States Council. The purpose is to coordinate and supervise the import and export operations in this business, to maintain business order and protect fair competition, to safeguard the legitimate rights and interests of the state, the trade and the members and to promote the sound development of foreign trade in medicinal items.

As the organizer of the industry, the Chamber has the following principal functions and tasks:

a) Guiding, coordinating, supervising and offering consulting service to its members in business operations.
b) Studying the export plans and import situation of medicinal products and making proposals to the relevant government departments.
c) Referring the members' needs and proposals to responsible government departments.
d) Safeguarding the import and export trade order and the interests of member enterprises.
e) Coordinating price, market and clients of foreign trade of medicinal products as authorized by the government or agreements of member enterprises at the common request of its members.
f) Assisting responsible departments under the State Council to

guide and supervise the legal operation.

g) Studying conditions of the international market, laws and regulations, agreements, trade restrictions concerning the foreign trade of medicinal products, analyzing finance, interest rate and currency conditions, thus providing information and consultation service for member enterprises.

h) Organizing anti-dumping and countervailing cases against Chinese enterprises in this trade, investigating dumping and other unfair competition activities of foreign medicinal products and reporting to the government.

i) Authorized by responsible departments under the State council, implementing tendering of medicinal product quotas.

j) Organizing trade fairs and international fairs for medicinal products and coordinating its member's participation in trade fairs, exhibitions, international fairs both at home and abroad.

k) Organizing study tours overseas for its members to market their products, place orders, conduct technological exchanges and promote foreign trade operations and publicity of commodities.

l) Representing the industry in international organizations of the same industry, attending relevant international professional conferences and signing documents for cooperation, strengthening ties with corresponding national and regional organizations in other parts of the world, exchanging information and developing business cooperation.

m) Coordinating its members in tendering of overseas projects jointly.

n) Other responsibilities as authorized by responsible departments under the State Council or at the common request of its members' enterprises of agreements of the trade.

In view of its tasks, the chamber has set up under its administration several branches and coordinating groups along the lines of products, each responsible for coordinating and supervising the import and export of commodities in its own line and offering advice in this regard. The day-to-day operations of the chamber are presided over by the President, the vice Presidents and secretary-general. Its permanent organization, which is located in Beijing, consists of the Department of Traditional Chinese Medicines, Pharmaceutical Department, Legal Affairs department, Exhibition Department, Information Department, Membership Department and the Administrative Office, which handle specific routines within their own authority.

URL: *www.cccmhpie.org.cn* (official Chinese web site) or for the English version

www.mhpie.com.cn/english/en_about_02.htm.

4.0 STATE ADMINISTRATION
OF TRADITIONAL CHINESE MEDICINES (SATCM)

The State Administration of Traditional Chinese Medicine (SATCM) is a state bureau under the Ministry of Public Health. It is responsible for administrating Traditional Chinese Medicine and Pharmacology (TCMP), to inherit and develop the science of TCMP, and promote the development of TCMP undertakings. Its main duties include: formulating the guidelines, policies, laws, and regulations of TCMP; working out department rules and regulations and supervising their implementation; formulating and organizing to implement the developing strategies of TCMP, drawing up intermediate and long-term development projects and annual programs; supervising appropriation of special funds and loans, and emergency allocation of TCMP resources in cases of disasters, pestilence and for military requirements; guiding the therapy, nursing, rehabilitation and health care of traditional Chinese medicine, integration of traditional Chinese medicine and Western medicine and nationality medicine; supervising the production of and trade of the Chinese medicines; organizing personnel training, scientific research, technology development and protection of intellectual property rights; developing international scientific exchange and cooperation; and making plans on export and import of Chinese medicines. (See *www. cintcm.ac.cn/gam/e_index6.html*.)

For more information, see URL: *www.satcm.gov.cn* (official Chinese website) or

www.satcm.gov.cn/english_satcm/eindex.htm (English version).

C. SPECIFIC REQUIREMENTS

1.0 PRE-MARKET AUTHORIZATIONS

Article 25 of the Drug Administration Act of the PRC states that the department of the State Council responsible for administering health shall organize investigation into drugs already approved for production; where the efficacy of the drug is not reliable, the side-effects to a drug are great, or a drug is for any other reason harmful to people's health, the approval number shall be revoked. Where the approval number of a drug has been revoked, production and sale of the drug may not be continued; what has already been produced shall be burnt or disposed of under the supervision of the local department administering health

Since the *Drug Administration Act* of the PRC includes both pharmaceutical and Chinese medicine products, Traditional Chinese Medicine (TCM) preparations, Chinese crude drugs, etc., a broad interpretation of Article 25 of the *Drug Administration Act* of the PRC means that pre-market testing, evaluation, and approval occurs for Health Food Products, Pharmaceutical Drugs, and TCM including Chinese herbal medicines and TCM preparations.

2.0 PRACTICE AND STANDARD SYSTEMS FROM THE DRUG ADMINISTRATION ACT OF THE PRC

a) Good Manufacturing Practice (GMP)

Article 9 states that a drug manufacturing enterprise shall observe the Good Manufacturing Practices for Pharmaceutical Products (GMP), according to this Law promulgated by SDA. The drug administration department shall conduct certification on drug manufacturing enterprises according to the requirements of GMP, and issue a GMP certificate to a qualified drug manufacturing enterprise. SDA shall be responsible for the promulgation of the working rules and implementation procedures of GMP. (Note: SDA is now SFDA).

Web site information source is to be found at: www.lehmanlaw.com/lib/library/Laws_regulations/pharma/drug_admlaw.htm .

b) Good Supply Practice (GSP)

Very little information was listed for this area. No specific information could be found.

c) Good Sales Practice (GSP)

Article 16: A drug operation enterprise shall observe the Good Sales Practices for Pharmaceutical Products (GSP), which is formulated according to this Law by SFDA. The drug administration departments shall certify drug operation enterprises according to the requirements of GSP, and issue GSP certificates to qualified drug manufacturing enterprises. SFDA shall be responsible for the promulgation of the working rules and implementation procedures of GSP.

URL: www.lehmanlaw.com/lib/library/Laws_regulations/pharma/drug_admlaw.htm .

d) Good Agriculture Practice (GAP)

SFDA: Good Agriculture Practices for Traditional Chinese Medicinal Plants and Animals (Transitional).

Regulation BIO: SDA regulation; Order No. 32; Promulgation Date 2002-04-17; Effective Date : 2002-06-01. Contents of this regulation are:

- Chapter I: General provisions (Articles 1-3)
- Chapter II: Production Habitat and Ecological Environment (Articles 4-7)
- Chapter III: Idioplasm and Reproduction Material (Articles 7-10)
- Chapter IV: Cultivation and Cultivation Control (Articles 11-25)
- Chapter V: Harvesting and preliminary Processing (Articles 26-33)
- Chapter VI: Packaging, Transportation and Storage (Articles 34-39)
- Chapter VII: Quality Control (Articles 40-44)
- Chapter VIII: Personnel and Facilities (Articles 45-51)
- Chapter IX: Documentation (Article 52-54)
- Chapter X: Supplementary Provisions (Articles 55-57).

Note: Only Chinese documents were found as available and no English translations were found.

SFDA: Administrative Measures on the Accreditation of Good Agricultural Practice for Chinese Crude Drugs (Trial Implementation) and Standards for the Review and Accreditation of Good Agricultural Practice for Chinese Crude Drugs (Trial Implementation).

Regulation BIO: Directive; Document No. GuoshiyaoJianAn (2003) 251; Promulgation Date: 2003-09-19; Effective Date; 2003-11-01. Administrative Measures on the Accreditation of the Good Agricultural Practice for Chinese Crude Drugs (Trial Implementation) and Standards for the Review and Accreditation of the Good Agricultural Practice for Chinese Crude Drugs (Trial Implementation), as the guideline of the accreditation of the GAP for Chinese Crude Drugs will enter into effect as of November 1, 2003.

e) Good Laboratory Practice (GLP)

SFDA: Drug Good Laboratory Practices
Regulation BIO: SFDA Regulation; Order No. 2; Promulgation Date: 2003-08-06; Effective Date: 2003-09-01. The highlights of this regulation are:

- Article 1. The provisions are established for improving the quality of non-clinical laboratory studies on new drugs, for assuring the truthfulness, integrity and reliability of experimental data, and for ensuring drug safety for human use pursuant to the stipulations of the *Drug Control Law* of the PRC; *and*
- Article 2. The provisions shall be adapted to non-clinical laboratory studies for applications of drug registration. All non-clinical research organizations shall follow the provisions.

Contents of the regulation are:

- Chapter I: General Provisions (Articles 1-2)
- Chapter II: Organization and Personnel (Articles 3-7)
- Chapter III: Laboratory Facilities (Articles 3-7)
- Chapter IV: Instruments, Equipment and Experimental Supplies (Articles 15-20)
- Chapter V: Standard Operation Procedures (Article 21-24)
- Chapter VI: Study Implementation (Articles 25-35)
- Chapter VII: Data and Archives (Articles 36-40)
- Chapter VIII: Supervision, Inspection and Certification (Article 41-42)
- Chapter IX: Supplementary Provisions (Articles 43-45).

f) Good Clinical Practice (GCP)

SFDA: Drug Good Clinical Practice (CHINA GCP): Standardization of clinical drug trials, scientific and credible results, protects benefits and safety of trial subjects. This is pursuant to the *Drug Control Law* of the PRC.

Regulation BIO: SFDA Regulation; Order No. 13; Effective Date: 1999-09-01; Repeal Date: 2003-09-01. The highlights of this regulation are:

- The China GCP is formulated to ensure the clinical trial process is standardized, the results scientific and credible, and the rights, benefits and safety of trial subjects protected. It is established pursuant to the Drug Control Law of the People's Republic of China and referring to the international recognized principles (Declaration of Helsinki).

- The China GCP is standard regarding the whole process of clinical trials including protecting, designing, organizing, implementing, monitoring, auditing, recording, analyzing and reporting.
- The clinical trials of all drugs, in various phases, including human bio-availability or bio-equivalence study must be performed according to the China GCP Guidelines.
- The Quality Assurance regulations deal with all aspects to ensure scientific integrity in the clinical trials (Chapter XI-Quality Assurance).

g) Green Trade Standard of Importing and Exporting Medicinal Plants and Preparations (Green Signs).

In January 2002, the Green Trade Standard was adopted by the CCCMPHIE (China Chamber of Commerce of Medicines and Health Products Importers and Exporters) in cooperation with the International Fund for Animal Wildlife (IFAW) and the Chinese Medicine Association of Suppliers (CMAS) in the United Kingdom.

Information on the Green Trade Standard is given below. Regulations have been published in China requiring cultivators to follow certain practices that minimize pesticide use and residues. China also adopted the "Green Trade Standards of Importing and Exporting Medicinal Plants and Preparations," that provide for testing of organochlorine pesticides, among other tests (e.g., heavy metals, bacteria, aflatoxin). Still, some of the specific restrictions on pesticide use that are imposed in the United States by the United States Environmental Protection Agency (EPA), and other organizations, are not present in China. This means that some of the pesticides that are used in China on herbs are not permitted in the United States for those crops(even if permitted for other crops).

URL: *www.itmonline.org/arts/cleanhrb.htm*

Launching Traditional Medicine Certification and Eco-labelling-China and the United Kingdom

The IFAW and the Chinese Medicine Association of Suppliers (CMAS) in the United Kingdom have come together as partners to work toward the common goal of promoting the health and well-being of all species by employing protective standards for the production of Traditional Medicine (TM) products. Their goal is that the standards will provide basic international guidelines that will protect people

and wildlife by providing safe TM products. Similar IFAW efforts
are underway in California where they are co-sponsoring legislation
to establish a statewide "Eco-labelling" certification program. CMAS
is an association of TM vendors in the United Kingdom that have
organized to create a system of self-regulation in cooperation with
relevant local government bodies and interested non-governmental
organizations. IFAW and CMAS have set forth guidelines to protect
biodiversity and provide quality and safety assurances. In an effort
to protect biodiversity, CMAS has proclaimed a policy of refusing to
sell any products containing endangered species. To this end, CMAS
has designed a system of importation whereby all of their products
are imported through a bonded warehouse facility that allows open
access to Customs officials and Convention on International Trade in
Endangered Species (CITES) officials. This system provides a more
efficient method of regulation for both businesses and government
officials.

CMAS and the China Chamber of Commerce of Medicines and
Health Products Importers and Exporters signed a memorandum of
cooperation in January 2002 to implement a certification scheme for
traditional medicine products. In China it is known as the "Green
Label" and in the United Kingdom as the "Kitemark Scheme," the
program meets the requirements of China's "Green Trade Standards
of Importing and Exporting Medicinal Plants and Preparations," as
well as the standards of the United Kingdom's Medicine Control
Agency, Department of Health. These twin standards are designed
to ensure consistently high safety and quality for TM products. The
certification program will also comply with the regulations of the
Convention on International Trade in Endangered Species. There are
two stages to this program; the first focuses on certifying raw herbs
and the second stage will cover patented TM products. The CMAS,
the China Chamber of Commerce of Medicines and Health Products
Importers and Exporters and other partners will manage this scheme
as a Trust.

URL: *www.ifaw.org/ifaw/general/default.aspx?oid=11813* .

APPENDIX 11

UNITED KINGDOM

1.0   BACKGROUND

In the United Kingdom (UK), the Medicines and Healthcare Products Regulatory Agency is the organization which ensures that medicines, healthcare products and medical equipment meet appropriate standards of safety, quality, performance and effectiveness, and are used safely. The supply of medicinal products in the UK is regulated by the provision of the Medicines Act 1968 and associated EC legislation. It is unlawful for any medicinal product to be placed on the market in the UK except in accordance with a product licence, unless a relevant exemption applies (e.g., "named patient" use under Section 9 of the Act). The main regulatory web site for the Medicines and Healthcare Products Regulatory Agency is : *http://www.mhra.gov.uk* .

2.0   HERBAL MEDICINES

Section 132 of the Medicines Act 1968 defines a herbal remedy as a medicinal product consisting of a substance produced by subjecting a plant or plants to drying, crushing or any other process, or of a mixture whose sole ingredients are two or more substances so produced, or of a mixture whose sole ingredients are one or more substances so produced and water or some other inert substance. In the United Kingdom, herbal remedies that are industrially produced are

regulated as drugs. Herbal products that are not industrially manufactured and for which no therapeutic claim is made are excluded
from the drug definition and are not regulated as medicinal products. Products containing mixtures of botanicals with vitamins and/
or minerals are regulated as food supplements under food law.[3] At
present, the majority of herbal medicines on the UK market are sold
and supplied as unlicensed herbal remedies under a legal provision
dating back to 1968. There are a relatively limited number of licensed
herbal medicines on the UK market.

There are two alternative regulatory routes for herbal medicines:

Licensed herbal medicines: to receive a marketing authorisation (product licence), herbal medicines are required to meet safety,
quality and efficacy criteria in a similar manner to any other licensed
medicines.

Herbal remedies exempt from licensing requirements: the exemption applies where herbal remedies meet conditions set out in
Section 12 of the Medicines Act 1968. Under the terms of the Act,
herbal remedies in the UK are exempt from the requirement to obtain
a medicine licence under certain conditions: either the herbal remedy
must be made up on the premises from which they are supplied and
be prescribed after a one-to-one consultation (Section 12(1)) or, if it
is an over-the-counter (pre-prepared) remedy, then it must not make
any written therapeutic claims (Section 12(2)). In both cases the remedy must comprise only of plant materials. Because S12(1) remedies
are not industrially produced, control of their supply remains under UK not EU legislation. Consequently S12(1) will remain in force
when the Traditional Herbal Medicinal Products Directive becomes
law. This means that in the UK, herbal medicines that are made up on
the premises and sold after a one-to-one consultation will continue to
be exempt from licensing requirements under this S12(1) provision.

Under the main piece of European legislation regulating medicines, Directive 2001/83 EC, industrially produced herbal medicines
placed on the market are required - like any other medicinal product - to have a marketing authorisation, based on demonstration of
safety, quality and efficacy. The Directive on Traditional Herbal Medicinal Products, which amends 2001/83/EC, opens up an additional
route for such remedies, with a simplified registration scheme.

---

[3]   *Herbal Medicine: Chaos in the Marketplace*, Rowena K. Ritcher, The
Haworth Herbal Press, 2003)

3.0   HOMEOPATHIC MEDICINES

A homoeopathic medicinal product is defined in European legislation (Article 1 Directive 92/73EEC) as any medicinal product prepared from products, substances or composition called homoeopathic stocks in accordance with a homoeopathic manufacturing procedure described by the European Pharmacopoeia or, in the absence thereof, by the pharmacopoeias currently used officially in the Member States. The homoeopathic registration scheme, implemented under a European Directive 92/73 EEC, is a simplified regulatory procedure, whereby products are assessed for their quality and safety and can then be marketed without specific medical claims. The simplified registration scheme thus enables a rapid introduction of new homoeopathic medicines onto the UK market. Registration under the scheme is compulsory only in respect of homoeopathic products new to the UK market. Products that were previously on the market by virtue of the Product Licenses Right (PLR) continue to be available.

In order to qualify for registration the products must:
a)   be for oral or external use. This includes all methods of administration with the exception of injections;
b)   be sufficiently diluted to guarantee their safety; and
c)   make no therapeutic claims.

In the UK, there is a simplified regulatory procedure which enables companies to market certain homoeopathic medicinal products in the UK. The basis for the scheme is set out in the Homoeopathics Directive 92/73/EEC. This was incorporated into UK law on 14 February 1994 and widens the scope of existing legislation in a move toward harmonization of the manufacture, control and supply of homoeopathic products within the EC. Under the provisions of the Medicines Act, a product licence may only be granted where satisfactory evidence of safety, quality and efficacy has been established. No new product licences have been granted for homoeopathic products since the Act came into force in 1971, although there are a considerable number of such products marketed under PLR which were allowed in respect of products already on the market when the Act was brought into force.

4.0   FOOD SUPPLEMENTS

In the United Kingdom food supplements are regulated by the Food Standards Agency.

Directive 2002/46/EC, which harmonises European Community

legislation on food supplements, defines the term "food supple-ments", provides a list of vitamin and mineral sources that may be used in the manufacture of food supplements, sets out labelling re-quirements and provides a framework for maximum and minimum levels for vitamins and minerals in food supplements to be set in the future. The Directive came into force on 12 July 2002 and was implemented in UK law by 31 July 2003. The Directive will not im-mediately outlaw any products already on the UK market. The Di-rective gives Member States the opportunity to allow continued sale of products containing vitamin and mineral sources not yet on the permitted list for up to seven years after the Directive comes into force, pending safety assessment of these sources.In the Food Sup-plement (England) Regulations 2003, recently enacted, "food supple-ment" means any food the purpose of which is to supplement the normal diet and which:

a) is a concentrated source of a vitamin or mineral or other sub-stance with a nutritional or physiological effect, alone or in combination; and

b) is sold in dose form.

5.0 VITAMINS AND MINERALS

The EU directive on food supplements became law in the UK on 31 July 2003. The Directive covers the composition (limited at present to the vitamins and minerals that can be included) and labelling of food supplements. It also establishes a framework for setting maxi-mum levels for vitamins and minerals in food supplements.

Directive 65/65/EEC sets out the definition of what is a medicine. This applies equally to herbal products as to any other kind of prod-uct. Many supplements consisting wholly or partly of herbal ingredi-ents on the UK market are not classified as medicines and can legally be sold under food laws.Vitamin and mineral supplements regulated as foods are subject to the general provisions of food laws, including the Food Safety Act 1990 and the Food Labelling Regulations 1996. The Act broadly requires food to be safe, of the nature, substance or quality demanded by the consumer, and makes it an offence to sell food which is falsely or misleadingly described or labelled. The Reg-ulations lay down detailed labelling requirements, including specific criteria which must be met if a supplement claims to be a source of vitamins/minerals, and prohibit medicinal claims. Supplements for which medicinal claims are made (to treat, prevent or cure disease) or which are administered to restore, correct or modify physiological function, fall within the definition of a medicine.

6.0 Site Licensing

Medicinal products manufactured in the UK must be produced on a site that holds an appropriate manufacturer's licence (ML). Any company or individual wishing to wholesale deal (defined as selling, supplying or procuring to anyone other than the end-user) medicinal products within the EU must hold a wholesale dealer's licence (WL). The administrative activities for issuing and maintaining manufacturer's licences and WLs are carried out by the Licensing Section in the Inspection and Enforcement Division of the Medicines and Healthcare Products Regulatory Agency (MHRA).

7.0 Good Manufacturing Practices (GMP)

Good Manufacturing Practices (GMPs) are part of quality assurance that ensures that medicinal products are consistently produced and controlled to the quality standards appropriate to their intended use and as required by the marketing authorisation (MA) or product specification. GMPs are concerned with both production and quality control. In 1991 requirements for manufacturing authorisations and GMP were harmonised within the European Community. The UK no longer inspected or exchanged Pharmaceutical Inspection Convention (PIC) reports on manufacturers in other EC Member States. Inspections are regulated in accordance with two Directives laying down the principles and guidelines of GMP, one for medicinal products for human use (Directive 91/356/EEC of 13 June 1991), the other for veterinary medicinal products (Directive 91/412/EEC of 23 July 1991).

Directive 91/356/EEC sets out the "principles and guidelines of Good Manufacturing Practice for medicinal products" mentioned in Article 19a of Directive 75/319/EEC. The detailed guidelines are published by the European Commission in the "Guide to Good Manufacturing Practice for Medicinal Products." These guidelines are available from the MHRA Information Centre. The European Commission is preparing an Annex containing supplementary guidance for manufacturers of homoeopathic products.

Holders of manufacturer(s) licences are required to:

a) establish and implement an effective pharmaceutical quality assurance system;

b) provide and maintain an independent quality control department, under the authority of the person nominated as responsible for overall quality control;

c) retain records and samples of starting materials and finished products for the required period; and

d) maintain an effective system whereby complaints are reviewed and products may be recalled.[4]

Site Inspection

Article 26 of Directive 75/319/EEC requires the Licensing Authority to ensure, by inspection at appropriate intervals, that licence holders are complying with the legal requirements. Inspectors are empowered to inspect all authorized sites, to take samples and to examine all relevant documents. Following an inspection, the licence holder will receive a copy of the Inspector's Reports.

8.0 ADVERSE REACTIONS REPORTING

In the UK, there is a Yellow Card Scheme which invites reports from doctors, dentists, coroners, pharmacists and nurses on adverse drug reactions. Reports are not accepted directly from patients as medical interpretation of the suspected reaction is considered vital. Patients who suspect they have suffered an adverse reaction to their medicines should report these to their doctor, pharmacist or nurses who may then report it to the Scheme. Although some herbal medicines are licensed for use, there are many herbal remedies available from outlets other than pharmacies, or supplied by herbal practitioners which are not licensed. All herbal products are monitored to ensure their safety and reports are invited on all suspected adverse reactions to any herbal remedy. Reporters are encouraged to provide as much information as possible about the remedy, including its ingredients, source or supplier, if known, and what the product was being used for. If the remedy was supplied by a herbal practitioner, the reporting of the name and is considered useful but not required. A sample of the product may be retained if the reaction is severe, in case further investigations need to be carried out.

---

4   *The Homeopathic Registration Scheme: Guidance for Manufacturers and Suppliers*, MHRA, September 2003)

APPENDIX 12

THE UNITED STATES OF AMERICA

1.0   DEFINITION OF A DIETARY SUPPLEMENT

The United States Congress defined the term "dietary supplement" in the Dietary Supplement Health and Education Act (DSHEA) of 1994. A dietary supplement is a product taken by mouth that contains a "dietary ingredient" intended to supplement the diet. The "dietary ingredients" in these products may include: vitamins, minerals, herbs or other botanicals, amino acids, and substances such as enzymes, organ tissues, glandulars, and metabolites. Dietary supplements can also be extracts or concentrates, and may be found in many forms such as tablets, capsules, softgels, gelcaps, liquids, or powders. They can also be in other forms, such as a bar, but if they are, information on their label must not represent the product as a conventional food or a sole item of a meal or diet. Whatever their form may be, DSHEA places dietary supplements in a special category under the general category of "foods," not drugs, and requires that every supplement be labelled a dietary supplement. The United States Food and Drug Administration (FDA) web site covering DSHEA is at _www.cfsan.fda.gov/_ .

A "New Dietary Ingredient" in a Dietary Supplement

The Dietary Supplement Health and Education Act (DSHEA) of

1994 defined both of the terms "dietary ingredient" and "new dietary ingredient" as components of dietary supplements. For an ingredient of a dietary supplement to be a "dietary ingredient," it must be one or any combination of the following substances:

- a vitamin;
- a mineral;
- a herb or other botanical;
- an amino acid;
- a dietary substance for use by man to supplement the diet by increasing the total dietary intake (e.g., enzymes or tissues from organs or glands); or
- a concentrate, metabolite, constituent or extract.

A "new dietary ingredient" is one that meets the above definition for a "dietary ingredient" and was not sold in the United States in a dietary supplement before October 15, 1994.

2.0 PRODUCT LICENSING:
FDA'S ROLE IN REGULATING DIETARY SUPPLEMENTS VERSUS THE MANUFACTURER'S RESPONSIBILITY FOR MARKETING THEM

In October 1994, the *Dietary Supplement Health and Education Act* (DSHEA) was signed into law. Before that time, dietary supplements were subject to the same regulatory requirements as were other foods. The new law, which amended the *Federal Food, Drug, and Cosmetic Act*, created a new regulatory framework for the safety and labelling of dietary supplements.

Under DSHEA, a firm is responsible for determining that the dietary supplements it manufactures or distributes are safe and that any representations or claims made about them are substantiated by adequate evidence to show that they are not false or misleading. This means that dietary supplements do not need approval from the FDA before they are marketed and are therefore not licenced. Except in the case of a new dietary ingredient, where pre-market review for safety data and other information is required by law, a firm does not have to provide the FDA with the evidence it relies on to substantiate safety or effectiveness before or after it markets its products.

3.0 DIETARY SUPPLEMENT CLAIMS

The FDA receives many consumer inquiries about the validity of claims for dietary supplements, including product labels, advertisements, media and printed materials. *There are three categories of claims that can be used on foods and dietary supplement labels: health claims, structure/function claims, and nutrient content claims.* The responsibility for ensuring the validity of these claims rests with the manufacturer, the FDA, or, in the case of advertising, with the Federal Trade Commission.

Health Claims for Dietary Supplements

The FDA receives many consumer inquiries about the validity of claims for dietary supplements, including product labels, advertisements, media, and printed materials. The responsibility for ensuring the validity of these claims rests with the manufacturer, The FDA, and, in the case of advertising, with the Federal Trade Commission. By law, manufacturers may make three types of claims for their dietary supplement products: health claims, structure/function claims, and nutrient content claims. Some of these claims describe: the link between a food substance and disease or a health-related condition, the intended benefits of using the product, and/or the amount of a nutrient or dietary substance in a product. Different requirements generally apply to each type of claim.

A statement or "disclaimer" is required by law (DSHEA) when a manufacturer makes a structure/function claim on a dietary supplement label. In general, these claims describe the role of a nutrient or dietary ingredient intended to affect the structure or function of the body. The manufacturer is responsible for ensuring the accuracy and truthfulness of these claims; they are not approved by the FDA. For this reason, the law says that if a dietary supplement label includes such a claim, it must state in a "disclaimer" that the FDA has not evaluated this claim. The disclaimer must also state that this product is not intended to "diagnose, treat, cure or prevent any disease," because only a drug can legally make such a claim. This is the reason for some supplements having wording (a disclaimer) that says: "This statement has not been evaluated by the FDA. This product is not intended to diagnose, treat, cure, or prevent any disease."

Legality of marketing a dietary supplement product as a treatment or cure for a specific disease or condition

A product sold as a dietary supplement and promoted on its label or in labelling as a treatment, prevention or cure for a specific disease or condition would be considered an unapproved drug and therefore illegal. Labelling refers to the label as well as accompanying material that is used by a manufacturer to promote and market a specific product. To maintain the product's status as a dietary supplement, the label and labelling must be consistent with the provisions in the *Dietary Supplement Health and Education Act* (DSHEA) of 1994.

Health Claims Based on Authoritative Statements

In 1997, the *Food and Drug Administration Modernization Act* (FDAMA) provided a second way for a health claim to be used on foods. It allows certain health claims to be made as a result of a successful submission of a notification based on an "authoritative statement" from a scientific body of the United States Government or the National Academy of Sciences. There is a separate guidance document that explains how a firm can make these types of health claims. It can be found at: http://www.cfsan.fda.gov/~dms/hclmguid.html. Congress did not include dietary supplements in the provisions for health claims based on authoritative statements. Consequently, this method of oversight for health claims cannot be used for dietary supplements at this time.

Qualified Health Claims

This kind of health claim was provided for by the FDA as a result of the U.S. Court of Appeals for the D.C. Circuit 1999 decision in the case of Pearson v. Shalala [64 F.3d 650 (D.C. Cir. 1999)]. This court decision, which focused on dietary supplements, specified that when the link between the substance's ability to reduce the risk of the disease does not meet the standard of "significant scientific agreement," the FDA can allow appropriately qualified health claims that would be misleading without such qualification. These qualified claims are based on the weight of the scientific evidence, i.e., there is more evidence for than against the relationship, but need not reach the standard of significant scientific agreement.

Structure / Function Health Claims

DSHEA created another category of statements, generally referred to as "structure/function" claims, that may be made for dietary supplements. These statements may claim a benefit related to a nutrient deficiency disease (like vitamin C and scurvy), as long as the statement also tells how widespread such a disease is in the United States. Structure/function claims may also describe the role of a nutrient or dietary ingredient intended to affect a structure or function in humans, for example, "calcium builds strong bones." In addition, they may characterize the means by which a nutrient or dietary ingredient acts to maintain such structure or function, for example, "fibre maintains bowel regularity," or "antioxidants maintain cell integrity," or they may describe general well-being from consumption of a nutrient or dietary ingredient. The manufacturer is responsible for ensuring the accuracy and truthfulness of these claims; they are not approved by the FDA. For this reason, the law says that if a dietary supplement label includes such a claim, it must state in a "disclaimer" that the FDA has not evaluated the claim. The disclaimer must also state that the dietary supplement product is not intended to "diagnose, treat, cure or prevent any disease," because only a drug can legally make such a claim. Manufacturers of dietary supplements that make structure/function claims on labels or in labelling must submit a notification to the FDA no later than 30 days after marketing the dietary supplement that includes the text of the structure/function claim.

Nutrient Content Claims

Under NLEA, foods and dietary supplements can use claims called "nutrient content claims." These claims describe the level of a nutrient or dietary substance in the product, using terms such as "good source," "high," or "free." Nutrient content claims may only be made if the FDA has a regulation specifying the criteria that a food must meet in order to use the claim. With few exceptions, nutrient content claims can only be made for nutrients or dietary substances that have an established daily value. The requirements that govern the use of nutrient content claims help ensure that descriptive terms, such as "high" or "low," are used consistently for all types of food products and are thus meaningful to consumers.

As was done for health claims, the *Food and Drug Administration Modernization Act* (FDAMA) of 1997 provided a second way for a nutrient content claim to be used on foods. FDAMA allows certain nutrient content claims to be made based on an "authoritative statement" as discussed above for health claims. However, these claims may be made for both conventional foods and dietary supplements. There is a separate guidance document, posted on the FDA's Web site, that explains how manufacturers can make these claims. Percentage claims for dietary supplements represent yet another category of nutrient content claims. These claims are used to describe a percentage level of a dietary ingredient for which there is no established Daily

Value. Examples include simple percentage statements such as "40% omega-3 fatty acids, 10 mg per capsule," and comparative percentage claims, e.g., "twice the omega-3 fatty acids per capsule (80 mg) as in 100 mg of menhaden oil (40 mg)."

4.0   GOOD MANUFACTURING PRACTICES

Manufacturers do not need to register themselves nor their dietary supplement products with the FDA before producing or selling them. Currently, there are no FDA regulations that are specific to dietary supplements that establish a minimum standard of practice for manufacturing dietary supplements. However, the FDA intends to issue regulations on good manufacturing practices that will focus on practices that ensure the identity, purity, quality, strength and composition of dietary supplements. At present, the manufacturer is responsible for establishing its own manufacturing practice guidelines to ensure that the dietary supplements it produces are safe and contain the ingredients listed on the label.

Manufacturing of "New Dietary Ingredient"

The *Dietary Supplement Health and Education Act* (DSHEA) requires that a manufacturer or distributor notify the FDA if it intends to market a dietary supplement in the U.S. that contains a "new dietary ingredient." The manufacturer (and distributor) must demonstrate to the FDA why the ingredient is reasonably expected to be safe for use in a dietary supplement, unless it has been recognized as a food substance and is present in the food supply.

There is no authoritative list of dietary ingredients that were marketed before October 15, 1994. Therefore, manufacturers and distributors are responsible for determining if a dietary ingredient is "new," and if it is not, for documenting that the dietary supplements it sells, containing the dietary ingredient, were marketed before October 15, 1994.

The FDA does not routinely analyze the content of Dietary Supplements. In that the FDA has limited resources to analyze the composition of food products, including dietary supplements, it focuses these resources first on public health emergencies and products that may have caused injury or illness. Enforcement priorities then go to products thought to be unsafe or fraudulent or in violation of the law. The remaining funds are used for routine monitoring of products pulled from store shelves or collected during inspections of manufacturing firms. The agency states that it does not analyze dietary supplements before they are sold to consumers. The manufacturer is responsible for ensuring that the "Supplement Facts" label and ingredient list are accurate, that the dietary ingredients are safe, and that the content matches the amount declared on the label. The FDA stated that it does not have resources to analyze dietary supplements sent to the agency by consumers who want to know their content. Instead, consumers may contact the manufacturer or a commercial laboratory for an analysis of the content.

FDA Proposes Labelling and Manufacturing Standards for Dietary Supplements

The FDA proposed current good manufacturing practice (CGMP) regulations for dietary ingredients and dietary supplements on April 29, 2003. The proposed rule would establish the minimum CGMPs necessary to ensure that, if you engage in activities related to manufacturing, packaging, or holding dietary ingredients or dietary supplements, you do so in a manner that will not adulterate and misbrand such dietary ingredients or dietary supplements. The provisions would require manufacturers to evaluate the identity, purity, quality, strength, and composition of their dietary ingredients and dietary supplements. The goal of this proposed rule is to promote and protect the public health.

Safety and Dietary Supplements

By law (DSHEA), the manufacturer is responsible for ensuring that its dietary supplement products are safe before they are marketed. Unlike drug products that must be proven safe and effective for their intended use before marketing, there are no provisions in the law for the FDA to "approve" dietary supplements for safety or effectiveness before they reach the consumer. Also unlike drug products, manufacturers and distributors of dietary supplements are not currently required by law to record, investigate or forward to the FDA any reports they receive of injuries or illnesses that may be related to the use of their products. Under DSHEA, once the product is marketed, the FDA has the responsibility for showing that a dietary supplement is "unsafe," before it can take action to restrict the product's use or removal from the marketplace. Manufacturers or distributors of dietary supplements do not have to tell the FDA or consumers what evidence they have about their product's safety or what evidence they have to back up the claims they are making for them.

Except for rules described above that govern "new dietary ingredients," there is no provision under any law or regulation that the FDA enforces that requires a firm to disclose to the FDA or consumers the information they have about the safety or purported benefits of their dietary supplement products. Likewise, there is no prohibition against them making this information available either to the FDA or to their customers. It is the responsibility of each firm to set its own policy on disclosure of such information.

The FDA's Oversight Responsibility for Dietary Supplements

As dietary supplements are under the category of foods, FDA's Center for Food Safety and Applied Nutrition (CFSAN) is responsible for the agency's oversight of these products. FDA's efforts to monitor the marketplace for potential illegal products (that is, products that may be unsafe or make false or misleading claims) include obtaining information from inspections of dietary supplement manufacturers and distributors, the Internet, consumer and trade complaints, occasional laboratory analyses of selected products, and adverse events associated with the use of supplements that are reported to the agency.

5.0   ADVERSE REACTION REPORTING

Reports of suspected adverse reactions to dietary supplements are made voluntarily.

If a person thinks that they have suffered a serious harmful effect or illness from a dietary supplement, their health care provider can report this by calling FDA's MedWatch hotline at 1-800-FDA-1088 or using the website. The MedWatch program allows health care providers to report problems possibly caused by FDA-regulated products such as drugs, medical devices, medical foods and dietary supplements. The identity of the patient is kept confidential.

As announced on August 29, 2002, the FDA, Center for Food Safety and Applied Nutrition (CFSAN), was developing a new, comprehensive system for tracking and analyzing adverse event reports involving foods, cosmetics and dietary supplements. This step is made possible in part by funds provided by Congress in our Fiscal Year 2002 appropriations. The new CFSAN Adverse Events Reporting System (CAERS) will eventually replace the patchwork of existing adverse event systems that were maintained by individual Offices within CFSAN. The agency will use the CAERS system as a monitoring tool to identify potential public health issues that may be associated with the use of a particular product already in the marketplace. Information gathered in CAERS will also assist the FDA in the formulation and dissemination of CFSAN's post-marketing policies and procedures.

As a first step in the CAERS roll-out, notification was made of a new process which will affect adverse event report processing by the Center. CFSAN will be writing a letter to notify companies that a report of an illness or injury allegedly associated with the use of one of their products was received by the Center. This letter notification is provided to companies for information, but it also allows the FDA to share its knowledge of an event concerning a company's product. To assist CFSAN in protecting consumer health, the FDA, in turn, encourages companies to share information with them that is relevant and useful concerning adverse events that companies may be aware of involving their product. The company letter notification process began for adverse event reports received on or after September 16, 2002.

On a related matter, CFSAN is currently evaluating under CAERS how best to provide adverse event data to the public on a user-friendly website. The current CFSAN website, the Special Nutritional Adverse Event Monitoring System for dietary supplements, has not been added to or updated since 1999. The information previously available on the dietary supplement website was very limited and was provided in a manner that made it difficult for users to appropriately interpret adverse events. Accordingly, that site has now been removed.

6.0   FORTIFIED FOOD

The United States FDA regulates the addition of vitamins and minerals to food through food standards and food additive regulations under the *Federal Food, Drug and Cosmetic Act* of 1938, as amended. These regulations control what nutrients can be added to food. Office of Food Additive Safety is responsible for the rules and regulations covering food and color additives (Title 21, Code of Federal Regulations).

The Center for Food Safety and Applied Nutrition, US Food and Drug Administration, United States Department of Health and Human Services is the regulatory agency that covers food standards including nutrient concerns such as vitamin D overdose.

7.0 HOMEOPATHIC DRUGS

Under the *Food, Drug and Cosmetics Act*, articles listed in the Homeopathic Pharmacopoeia of the United States are legally defined as drugs. When the Act was passed in 1938, these articles were essentially grand-fathered into the definition of a drug. However, drugs listed in the Homeopathic Pharmacopoeia of the United States continue to be exempt from pre-market FDA review of safety and efficacy. Products that are sold as homeopathic remedies must comply with the specifications set out in the Homeopathic Pharmacopoeia of the United States and relevant regulations. A homeopathic drug product may not contain any non-homeopathic active ingredients and therefore is rarely formulated in combination with dietary supplements.

The Food and Drug Administration sets out the conditions under which homeopathic drugs may be marketed in the U.S. at the following web site: *http://www.fda.gov/ora/compliance_ref/cpg/cpgdrg/cpg400-400.html* .

Printed in the United States
134030LV00007BA/201/P